Stan Williamson, PhD
Robert E. Stevens, PhD
David L. Loudon, PhD
R. Henry Migliore, PhD

Fundamentals of Strategic Planning for Healthcare Organizations

Pre-publication
REVIEWS,
COMMENTARIES,
EVALUATIONS . . .

"The authors have written an extremely readable, useful reference for healthcare strategic planners. The text provides an excellent overview of the strategic planning process for healthcare managers.

The volume is complete with numerous examples of healthcare strategic planning documents that executive team members should find very useful in managing the strategic planning process."

Michael M. Costello, JD
Vice President,
Corporate Development,
Moses Taylor Hospital,
Scranton, PA

More pre-publication
REVIEWS, COMMENTARIES, EVALUATIONS . . .

"Most books about strategic planning put hands-on managers to sleep. This is the exception. Williamson et al. have prepared a highly readable outline of 'critical pathways' for growing companies that need to formalize their decision-making.

The most useful parts of this text are the sample plans employed by actual operating healthcare firms as well as the form versions of such organizational documents as mission statements and evaluation and control sheets. The authors employ a step-by-step method to illustrate the practical components of strategic planning. This text would be excellent for any capstone MBA or executive development course that turns out real managers. Long on specifics, short on vague theorization, this is the text to keep the next time your library gets pruned."

Robert E. Sweeney, DA, MBA
Senior Vice President and Principal, Teamhealth, Memphis, TN

"This is a practical, succinct, and powerful overview of the strategic planning process, which can be of benefit to managers in large or small organizations. The book's strength is twofold: (1) it reduces complex and sometimes confusing concepts to simple, understandable steps; and (2) the information is practical and can be immediately incorporated into an organization's planning process.

The authors make the point throughout the book that the planning process is really a thinking process. Chapter 4 in particular drives home this point. The authors use an analytical framework they call SWOT, an acronym for strengths, weaknesses, opportunities, and threats, to guide readers through a systematic analysis of a health care organization's situation. They list factors to be used when assessing the external environment, and emphasize the importance of coming to grips with internal weaknesses as well as strengths. The roles of marketing and communication are also woven nicely into the strategic planning process.

The book is packed with worksheets, lists to guide the reader through the necessary planning steps, and samples of comprehensive strategic planning documents of actual healthcare organizations."

Jim McBride, MS
Director of Public Affairs and Communications, Kaiser Permanente Medical Care Program, San Diego, CA

More pre-publication
REVIEWS, COMMENTARIES, EVALUATIONS . . .

"This book is both an excellent primer in healthcare strategic planning as well as a ready reference for the experienced planner. The text is eminently readable, yet full of valuable information presented in a format that is both logical and progressive. Drs. Williamson, Stevens et al. have done a masterful job of laying out the essentials of the strategic planning process for healthcare, focusing not only on the 'How tos' but also the 'Whys.' They also bring insight into the planning process from other industries.

In my opinion, the worksheets included at the end of each chapter are probably the most beneficial sections of the book, particularly when it comes to generating one's own strategic plan. These worksheets, combined with the probing questions included along the way, provide a structured process to follow in the development of a solid foundation for planning. The sample strategic plans that are found in the Appendixes are also of great value for their idea-generating potential."

John M. Chamberlain, MHA
Associate Administrator
for Operations, Medical Center Hospital,
Odessa, TX

"The authors have written a very comprehensive and readable book on what strategic planning is and how to implement the process in healthcare organizations. The chapters move logically and thoroughly from perspectives and overview of strategic planning all the way through evaluation and control procedures. The content is highly relevant and inclusive, with all elements of the strategic planning model considered.

Additionally, this book is very 'user-friendly.' Healthcare managers who are new to the concept will find the ample inclusion of worksheets and sample strategic plans to be especially helpful. Any healthcare managers who find themselves having to develop a strategic plan for the first time will find this volume especially valuable."

Stephen O'Connor, PhD
Associate Professor of Health
Care Management,
School of Business Administration,
University of Wisconsin-Milwaukee

The Haworth Press, Inc.

NOTES FOR PROFESSIONAL LIBRARIANS AND LIBRARY USERS

This is an original book title published by The Haworth Press, Inc. Unless otherwise noted in specific chapters with attribution, materials in this book have not been previously published elsewhere in any format or language.

CONSERVATION AND PRESERVATION NOTES

All books published by The Haworth Press, Inc. and its imprints are printed on certified ph neutral, acid free book grade paper. This paper meets the minimum requirements of American National Standard for Information Sciences–Permanence of Paper for Printed Material, ANSI Z39.48-1984.

Fundamentals of Strategic Planning for Healthcare Organizations

HAWORTH Marketing Resources
Innovations in Practice & Professional Services
William J. Winston, Senior Editor

New, Recent, and Forthcoming Titles:

Market Analysis: Assessing Your Business Opportunities by Robert E. Stevens, Philip K. Sherwood, and J. Paul Dunn

Selling Without Confrontation by Jack Greening

Persuasive Advertising for Entrepreneurs and Small Business Owners: How to Create More Effective Sales Messages by Jay P. Granat

Marketing Mental Health Services to Managed Care by Norman Winegar and John L. Bistline

New Product Screening: A Step-Wise Approach by William C. Lesch and David Rupert

Church and Ministry Strategic Planning: From Concept to Success by R. Henry Migliore, Robert E. Stevens, and David L. Loudon

Business in Mexico: Managerial Behavior, Protocol, and Etiquette by Candace Bancroft McKinniss and Arthur A. Natella

Managed Service Restructuring in Health Care: A Strategic Approach in a Competitive Environment by Robert L. Goldman and Sanjib K. Mukherjee

A Marketing Approach to Physician Recruitment by James Hacker, Don C. Dodson, and M. Thane Forthman

Marketing for CPAs, Accountants, and Tax Professionals edited by William J. Winston

Strategic Planning for Not-for-Profit Organizations by R. Henry Migliore, Robert E. Stevens, and David L. Loudon

Marketing Planning in a Total Quality Environment by Robert E. Linneman and John L. Stanton, Jr.

Managing Sales Professionals: The Reality of Profitability by Joseph P. Vaccaro

Squeezing a New Service into a Crowded Market by Dennis J. Cahill

Publicity for Mental Health Clinicians: Using TV, Radio, and Print Media to Enhance Your Public Image by Douglas H. Ruben

Managing a Public Relations Firm for Growth and Profit by A. C. Croft

Utilizing the Strategic Marketing Organization: The Modernization of the Marketing Mindset by Joseph P. Stanco

Internal Marketing: Your Company's Next Stage of Growth by Dennis J. Cahill

The Clinician's Guide to Managed Behavioral Care by Norman Winegar

Marketing Health Care into the Twenty-First Century: The Changing Dynamic by Alan K. Vitberg

Fundamentals of Strategic Planning for HealthCare Organizations edited by Stan Williamson, Robert E. Stevens, David L. Loudon, and R. Henry Migliore

Risky Business: Managing Employee Violence in the Workplace by Lynne Falkin McClure

Fundamentals of Strategic Planning for Healthcare Organizations

Stan Williamson, PhD
Robert E. Stevens, PhD
David L. Loudon, PhD
R. Henry Migliore, PhD

The Haworth Press
New York • London

The Haworth Press, Inc., 10 Alice Street, Binghamton, NY 13904-1580

Library of Congress Cataloging-in-Publication Data

Fundamentals of strategic planning for healthcare organizations / Stan Williamson . . . [et al.].
p. cm.
Includes bibliographical references and index.
ISBN: 0-7890-0060-1
1. Health services administration. 2. Strategic planning. I. Williamson, Stan.
RA971.F86 1996
362.1'1'068–dc20

95-43398
CIP

CONTENTS

About the Authors ix

Preface xi

Acknowledgments xiii

Chapter 1. Planning Perspectives 1

Healthcare Organizations 4
Planning Is Important 5
What Is Planning? 7
Types of Plans 7
Advantages of Planning for Healthcare Organizations 8
Planning's Place in the Healthcare Organization 11
Resistance to the Planning Process 12
Revenue Source Influences on Planning 15
The Greatest Needs of Today's Healthcare Organizations 16
Summary 19

Chapter 2. Overview of Strategic Planning 21

What Is Strategic Planning? 21
The Strategic Planning Process 22
Strategic Planning As an Ongoing Process 30
Strategy Implementation 30
Summary 31
Planning Process Worksheet 32

Chapter 3. Defining Organizational Purpose 35

The Importance of Defining Purpose 35
Basic Elements of an Effective Mission Statement 37
Writing a Statement of Purpose 39
Sample Mission Statements 41
Evaluating a Purpose Statement 47

Vision Statements 48
Summary 50
Mission and Vision Statements Worksheet 51

Chapter 4. Situation Analysis and Assumptions **55**

External Analysis 55
Internal Analysis 61
Using a SWOT Analysis 66
Making Assumptions 69
Summary 71
Situation Analysis and Assumptions Worksheet 73

Chapter 5. Establishing Organizational Objectives **87**

Nature and Role of Objectives 87
Alternatives to Management by Objectives 90
Characteristics of Good Objectives 91
Types of Objectives Included in a Strategic Plan 95
Using Environmental Analysis Data to Set Objectives 98
Performance Contracts 100
Periodic Review 100
Summary 105
Objectives Worksheet 106

Chapter 6. Developing Strategy and Operational Plans **109**

Strategy Concepts 109
Alternative Strategies 110
Factors Influencing Strategy Selection 116
Operational Plans 117
Summary 121
Strategy Development Worksheet 124

Chapter 7. Evaluation and Control Procedures **129**

Integration of Planning and Control 130
Performance Evaluation and Control 132
Establishing Procedures 136
Performance Evaluation Guidelines 136
Summary 137

Conclusion 138
Evaluation and Control Worksheet 140

APPENDIXES

Appendix A. Strategic Planning Worksheets and Strategic Plan Outline 145
Planning Process Worksheet 147
Mission and Vision Statements Worksheet 149
Situation Analysis and Assumptions Worksheet 152
Objectives Worksheet 166
Strategy Development Worksheet 168
Evaluation and Control Worksheet 173
Strategic Plan Outline 175

Appendix B. Sample Strategic Plans 177
Healthcare Department of a State Penitentiary 179
Medical Clinic 185
Managed Care Department of a Medical Clinic 199
Operations Department of a Medical Clinic 205
Regional Medical Center 211
Metropolitan Medical Center 231

Appendix C. Sample Questionnaires 243

Index 257

ABOUT THE AUTHORS

Stan Williamson, PhD, is Associate Professor of Management at Northeast Louisiana University. He teaches strategic management, human resource management, and principles of management. Dr. Williamson received a PhD in Organizational Behavior/Personnel Management from the University of North Texas, an MS in Health Care Administration from Trinity University (Texas), and a BS in Business Administration from Louisiana Tech University. He is the author of two books and more than 20 articles. Dr. Williamson has 14 years of experience as a senior executive in a large regional healthcare system and has served as a management consultant in the field.

Robert E. Stevens, PhD, is Professor of Marketing at Northeast Louisiana University. He teaches marketing research, marketing management, statistics, strategic management, and principles of marketing. He holds a PhD in Marketing from the University of Arkansas and is the author of 11 books and more than 100 articles. Dr. Stevens has served as a consultant to local, regional, and national firms for research projects, feasibility studies, and market planning, and has been a partner in a marketing research company.

David L. Loudon, PhD, is Professor of Marketing and Head of the Department of Management and Marketing in the College of Business Administration at Northeast Louisiana University. He holds a PhD in Marketing from Louisiana State University and is the author of over 50 articles and seven books on topics such as consumer behavior, marketing and strategic planning. Dr. Loudon has conducted research in the United States, Europe, Asia, and Latin America on a variety of topics, including the application of marketing concepts to nontraditional areas. He has served as a consultant and is president of a computer software firm.

R. Henry Migliore, PhD, is Professor of Strategic Planning and Management at Northeastern University/University Center at Tulsa, where he teaches both graduate and undergraduate courses. He was formerly Dean of the Oral Roberts University School of Business. He is heavily involved in consulting for national and multinational firms. He is the author of numerous articles and books, including *An MBO Approach to Long-Range Planning, Strategic Long-Range Planning,* and *Strategic Planning and Management.*

Preface

Three primary considerations were used in preparing this book. The first was length. We wanted to keep the amount of reading material brief enough to be read and reviewed quickly. Therefore, only essential concepts and techniques are presented, and only in a very concise form.

The second consideration was to present material that is theoretically sound but practically oriented. We wanted the reader to be able to put the concepts presented to immediate use in decision making. We have also included chapter-end worksheets (which are also conveniently grouped in Appendix A) to help readers develop their own strategic plans.

The final consideration was to provide a thorough set of appendixes to illustrate various aspects of strategic planning and sample strategic plans. Thus the reader will not only read about strategic planning but actually see what a strategic plan looks like. This is useful in evaluating plans prepared by others or in preparing your own.

The end result, we believe, is a book that is both readable and helpful to those involved with the administration of healthcare organizations. We hope the book will serve as both a tutorial and an easily accessible reference for readers.

Stan Williamson, PhD
Robert E. Stevens, PhD
David L. Loudon, PhD
R. Henry Migliore, PhD

Acknowledgments

A book is seldom the work of the authors alone but involves the efforts of a great number of people. We would specifically like to thank Carol Albright, who tirelessly typed the final versions of the manuscript, Rachel Farrar, who constructed the index, and the administration of Northeast Louisiana University, for their support of this project.

Chapter 1

Planning Perspectives

You've got to come up with a plan. You can't wish things will get better.

John F. Welch
CEO, General Electric

If you are struggling with any of the following problems or questions, this book may be very important to you:

- Why is there so much confusion among our vice presidents and department heads about what we are trying to accomplish?
- Why is there so much dissension and disagreement in this organization?
- Why is there such a high turnover of people in our organization, especially in leadership positions?
- Why did we spend money on new services when they are not being used?
- As CEO (chief executive officer) why am I working 12 hours a day, and can never keep up?
- Why have we been less than successful on a number of projects and programs?
- Why have our revenues dropped off?
- Why does this organization lack enthusiasm?
- Why has the Board asked me to resign after everything I have put into this organization?

If you are wrestling with any of these questions, the answer might be that your healthcare organization (HCO) lacks effective long-term strategic planning.

And you would be in good company. Consider the recent sagas of such organizations as Mercy Health System of Janesville, Wisconsin; UniHealth America; and Holy Cross Hospital of Chicago. What do these organizations have in common? They all are healthcare providers that have faced up to and successfully overcome declining levels of patient admissions/client enrollments and serious revenue shortfalls. Each of these organizations can attribute its newfound success to effective use of strategic plans.

Mercy Health System's patient loads had been declining for six consecutive years. The organization was barely making ends meet in the late 1980s. With survival at stake, Mercy developed a strategic plan, reenvisioning its mission with the hospital as the cornerstone of an integrated regional healthcare delivery system. Strategies were implemented that capitalized on Mercy's strengths, such as low debt, and worked on its weaknesses, such as its local reputation as a lightweight provider when it came to sophisticated medical services. With input from its employees, Mercy focused on adding tertiary services, new physician recruitment initiatives, and ambulatory care centers, all as part of a vertically integrated, managed care system.

Although Mercy prefers to measure its performance in terms of how well it has expanded its services to its region, with the system's new strategy the numbers are telling and dramatic. For 1989-1990, Mercy was struggling to make payroll on revenues of $33.5 million. By 1994, patient income had risen to $133 million.[1]

After systematic analysis, the predecessor organizations of UniHealth America realized the industry they sought to serve had developed into a highly competitive managed care environment with which they could no longer cope. Their world had changed, and they had not. In response, a merger helped overcome initial operating weaknesses and subsequent acquisitions of other facilities transformed UniHealth America into a thriving healthcare system with seven acute care hospitals, two psychiatric/substance dependency treatment facilities, and two health maintenance organizations (HMOs).

UniHealth America developed a strategic plan employing a combination of strategies, including retrenchment by major reductions in force early on. This was followed quickly by growth through acquisitions. Its fundamental competitive strategy became one of differentiating itself from its competitors. Distinctiveness was developed through its physician collaboration programs and major facility upgrades. UniHealth has also launched a comprehensive information system available by terminal to all system physicians. The system includes a patient database as a foundation for improving patient care outcomes and delivery efficiency.

Through these efforts a dramatic turnaround was achieved. From having only 37 days of operating cash in the premerger days, UniHealth America's first year under its strategic plan showed gross revenues of $1.7 billion with net profits of $14.8 million.[2]

Like the first two examples, Holy Cross Hospital of Chicago was in trouble in 1991, facing a net operating loss of $8.9 million for the year. Needing to turn the situation around, a short-term retrenching strategy was begun with major staffing cutbacks and renegotiated service contracts. But the real catalyst for change was the long-range strategic plan developed by the hospital's new CEO.

Holy Cross refocused its vision and values as an organization, invigorating a renewed mission to become the premier quality and service healthcare provider for their community. Seeking to become more client-driven, the hospital system found opportunities to meet the needs of its constituents by recruiting more primary care and obstetrics/gynecology physicians. Holy Cross also built more primary care clinics and a new physician office building and started a managed care program.

By involving the physicians and the employees in the strategic planning process, Holy Cross made a successful comeback, moving from the lowest 5 percent of U.S. hospitals by size in patient satisfaction to the top 5 percent. The numbers are there as well. The hospital reported net margins of $1.7 million in 1993 and $2.75 million in 1994–a very long way from its $7.8 million loss in 1991.[3]

In the past, traditional business enterprises were the primary users of strategic planning. Increasingly, however, healthcare providers such as these organizations have begun to apply strategic planning concepts to improve the effectiveness of their operations.

A recent study documented the potential improvement in operations when strategic planning is used. Fifty-one hospitals using strategic planning showed an average total margin of 3.16 percent, while 15 hospitals without such plans averaged –1.07 percent.[4]

Using the techniques described in this book, your organization can better position itself to increase its operational effectiveness as well.

HEALTHCARE ORGANIZATIONS

The typical profit-seeking firm relies almost solely on the sale of its goods or services to the public for its revenue. While many healthcare organizations share this fundamental characteristic, they tend to differ from the traditional business enterprise in several ways. Let's explore the differences:

1. Healthcare organizations provide services vital to society and to the individual at an immediate, fundamental level, often in nonpostponable situations. Beyond this social good, they also provide an economic good (currently estimated at about $900 billion for the U.S. economy[5]). The social and economic priorities of these services often conflict, presenting dilemmas with ethical ramifications.
2. Physicians control the amount and degree of much of the work output in HCOs, yet they remain largely outside management's control.
3. In addition to physicians, other credentialed professionals deliver services that are highly interdependent on one another. These professionals often hold allegiances more to their profession than to their employer, complicating managerial coordination efforts.
4. The work product must be highly individualized, often confounding managerial attempts to improve efficiency.
5. The quality of the work performed is difficult to evaluate. Just defining quality here is challenging.
6. The governmental, economic, technological, and social environments within which HCOs operate generate dynamic, highly complex, and often conflicting demands on the provider.

While none of these factors, taken alone, is necessarily unique to healthcare organizations, the confluence of all these characteristics make healthcare organizations among the most difficult to manage strategically.[6,7] In no other industry is management faced with satisfying the needs of such a wide constituency.

The mounting, even skyrocketing, cost of healthcare is a matter of deep concern in many sectors. In recognition of these concerns, new forms of healthcare delivery sprang up in the 1980s. Beginning with health maintenance organizations (HMOs), and then preferred provider organizations (PPOs), the healthcare landscape is newly littered with an increasing variety of delivery mechanisms intent, at heart, on lowering the costs of care. Trends indicate that managed care, encompassing these and other organizational forms, is rapidly becoming the dominant delivery technique for the 1990s. Here a single controlling arrangement integrates the financial aspects and healthcare delivery of a full spectrum of health service organizations from primary, preventive, and rehabilitative services to acute and long-term tertiary care.

Regardless of form of delivery, the healthcare industry's growth has been enormous. It is now the nation's third largest. But with this dramatic growth has come a volatility in the healthcare industry's structure that has left many providers reeling. Columbia Healthcare Corporation's $5.7 billion merger with Hospital Corporation of America to become the nation's biggest proprietary hospital chain and Lifetime Corporation's $2.2 billion alliance with Olsten Corporation to become the largest home healthcare organization in America are but two of the many dramatic mergers and acquisitions that have become commonplace in the 1990s.[8]

Despite these challenges, and maybe because of them, this book is designed specifically to aid today's healthcare organization in developing a strategic planning process to chart a successful course through a turbulent industry currently experiencing a sea change in its ways of doing business. If healthcare executives can use strategic planning in developing solutions, not only in the operation of the facility, but also in developing proper network relationships, as well as managed care strategies, it will be a giant stride in the move from a crisis situation to a results-oriented management system.

PLANNING IS IMPORTANT

Planning as part of the management process is crucial to the success of any organization. When you consider the nature of healthcare organizations in particular, this is especially true. The increasing volatility of the environments in which all organizations and especially HCOs must function has forced major changes in the scope of the planning process. No longer will it suffice simply to lay plans for internal operations. To adapt to ever-changing environmental forces, organizations have moved to strategic planning, with its greater emphasis on stretching the organization to maintain a proper fit between it and the demands of its environment.

Out of a large number of decisions made by an organization or by an individual HCO executive, there are a handful of critical ones that can significantly impact the future of the organization and its leadership. These strategic decisions require careful identification and thoughtful consideration. This is the nature of the role of strategic planning.

Strategic thinking perspectives can be illustrated with this metaphorical question: Who are the two most important persons responsible for the success of an airplane's flight? A typical response would be:

- the pilot and the navigator, or
- the pilot and the maintenance supervisor, or
- the pilot and the air traffic controller, or
- the pilot and the flight engineer.

All of these responses recognize the day-to-day hands-on importance of the pilot. They all introduce one of several other important support or auxiliary functionaries into the answer. However, each of these segmented responses ignores the one person who is perhaps the single most important individual to the ultimate success of the airplane-the designer. Perhaps the pilot and the designer are the two most important individuals to the success of an airplane–the pilot because of the day-to-day responsibilities in commanding the craft, and the designer because of the ability to create a concept that can be economically constructed, easily operated by any normally competent flight crew, and maintained safely by the ground crew.

Most contemporary administrators of healthcare entities perceive themselves as the "pilot" of their organizations: taking off, landing, conferring with the navigator, and communicating with the air traffic controller. They generally view themselves as the chief hands-on operational manager. However, what has been most lacking in these organizations in the past few years has been an appreciation for the strategic viewpoint. There is a need for more emphasis on the "designer" approach to operating a healthcare venture. A well-conceived strategic planning system can facilitate this emphasis.

A healthcare organization without a long-term planning perspective faces a tough situation. Instead of moving steadily toward its goals, the organization will continually swerve off course due to the endless supply of distractions that can prevent an HCO from pursuing its purpose and vision. As one of the keys to success of any undertaking, strategic planning can act as a guiding star to keep an organization on track, particularly when the way seems hard to find. Certainly nowhere is it more important than in healthcare organizations, where many are facing questions of survival.

WHAT IS PLANNING?

Planning may be defined as a managerial activity that involves determining your fundamental purpose as an organization, analyzing the environment, setting objectives, deciding on specific actions needed to reach the objectives, and then adapting the original plan as feedback on results is received. This process should be distinguished from the plan itself, which is a written document containing the results of the planning process. The plan is a written statement of what is to be done and how it is to be done. Planning is a continuous process that both precedes and follows other functions. Plans are made and executed, and results are used to make new plans as the process continues.

TYPES OF PLANS

There are many types of plans, but most can be categorized as either *strategic* or *tactical.* Strategic plans cover a long period of time and may be referred to as *long-term.* They are broad in scope and basically answer the question of how an organization is to commit its resources over the next three to five, possibly even ten, years. Strategic plans are altered on an infrequent basis to reflect changes in the environment or overall direction of the organization.

Tactical plans cover a short time period, usually a year or less. They are often referred to as *short-term* or *operational* plans. They specify what is to be done in a given year to move the organization toward its long-term objectives. In other words, what we do this year (short-term) needs to be tied to where we want to be five to ten years in the future (long-term).

Traditionally, HCOs that have been involved in planning have focused on short-term rather than long-term planning. This is better than no planning at all; but it also means each year's plan is not related to anything long-term in nature and usually falls short of moving the organization to where it wants to be in the future.

Programs and events require planning also. A *program* is a large set of activities involving a specific area of an HCO's capabilities, such as planning for a new outpatient surgery service or a new managed care system. Planning for programs involves:

1. Dividing the total set of activities into meaningful parts.
2. Assigning planning responsibility for each part to appropriate people.
3. Assigning target dates for completion of plans.
4. Determining and allocating the resources needed for each part.

Each major program or division within a healthcare organization should have a strategic plan in place to provide a blueprint for the program over time.

An *event* is generally a project of less scope and complexity. It is also not likely to be repeated on a regular basis. An event may be a part of a broader program, such as the grand opening of a day surgery service, or it may be self-contained, such as an annual health fair at the local mall. Even for a onetime event, planning is an essential element to accomplish the objectives of the project and coordinate the activities that make up the event.

ADVANTAGES OF PLANNING FOR HEALTHCARE ORGANIZATIONS

Why should an HCO devote time to planning? Consider the following questions:

- Do you know where you are going and how you are going to get there?
- Does everyone in the organization know what you are trying to accomplish?
- Does everyone in the organization know what is expected of them?

If the answer to any of these is no, then your HCO needs to develop a long-range plan with as many people involved as possible. Your plan has never been more crucial in the dynamic environment your organization faces. Strategic planning can guide your organization through decision making and actions that determine whether an enterprise prospers, survives, or fails.

In many small HCOs, administrators may object to planning, thinking that it makes no sense for them. Since theirs is only a small organization, everyone associated knows what happened in the past year and what is likely to happen in the coming year. Another objection often voiced is that there is no time for planning. A third objection is that there are not enough resources to allow for planning.

All these objections actually point out the necessity for planning even in the small healthcare firm. Such an organization may actually have a sizeable budget, making it imperative to have a plan for where the organization is heading. The feeling that there is no time for planning may seem accurate, but probably simply reflects the fact that the lack of planning in the past has left insufficient time for attention to such necessities. Finally, the argument that there are insufficient resources should justify the role of planning in order to obtain the maximum benefit from those resources being used in the organization. In sum, planning is a critical element in any healthcare organization's success.

Planning has many advantages. For example, it helps executives adapt to changing environments, take advantage of opportunities created by change, reach agreements on major issues, and place responsibility more precisely. It also gives a sense of direction to staff members as well as providing a basis for gaining their commitment. The sense of vision that can be provided in a well-written plan also instills a sense of loyalty in organization members or constituents.

An HCO can benefit from the planning process because it is a systematic, continuing process that allows it to:

1. Assess its market position. This involves what is termed a SWOT analysis-examining the healthcare entity's internal *s*trengths and *w*eaknesses and and external *o*pportunities and *t*hreats. Without explicit planning, these elements may go unrecognized.
2. Establish goals, objectives, priorities, and strategies to be completed within specified time periods. Planning will enable the HCO to assess accomplishment of the goals that are set and will help motivate administrative staff and professional constituencies to work together to achieve shared goals.
3. Achieve greater staff and employee commitment and teamwork aimed at meeting challenges and solving problems presented by changing conditions.
4. Muster its resources to meet these changes through anticipation and preparation. "Adapt or die" is a very accurate admonition.

Healthcare executives exert only limited control over their organizations' futures. But they can and should attempt to identify and isolate present actions and forecast how results can be expected to influence the future. The primary purpose of planning, then, is to see that current programs and findings can be used to increase the chances of achieving future objectives and goals; that is, to increase the chances of making decisions today that will enhance performance tomorrow.

Unless planning leads to improved performance, it is not worthwhile. Thus, to have a healthcare organization that looks forward to the future and tries to stay alive and prosper in a changing environment, there must be active, vigorous, continuous, and creative planning. Otherwise, the HCO will only react to its environment.

When you boil it down, there are basically two reasons for planning: (1) protective benefits resulting from reduced chances for error in decision making and (2) positive benefits in the form of increased success in reaching organizational objectives.

Some HCOs and their leaders who plan poorly, if at all, constantly devote their energies to solving problems that would not have existed, or at least would be much less serious, with planning. They spend their time fighting fires rather than practicing fire prevention.

Strategic (long-range) planning can become a means of renewal in the life of an organization if the following five significant points about planning are remembered:

1. A unified purpose can be achieved only when all segments of the healthcare organization see themselves as part of a larger whole with a single goal.
2. Isolated individual decisions and commitments often influence future plans, even when they are not intended to do so.
3. When careful planning is lacking, groups in the HCO often become competitive with one another and duplicate one another's work.
4. Without coordinated planning, organizational divisions in the HCO may come to feel they are ends in themselves and lose their sense of perspective in relation to the organization.
5. The magnitude of the tasks facing an HCO demand long-range planning.[9]

PLANNING'S PLACE IN THE HEALTHCARE ORGANIZATION

We are now ready to discuss who does the planning, or the place of planning in a healthcare organization. Obviously, all leaders engage in planning to some degree. As a general rule, the larger the healthcare organization becomes, the more the primary planning activities become associated with groups of people as opposed to individuals.

Many larger HCOs develop a planning committee or staff. Organizations set up such a planning team for one or more of the following reasons:

1. *Planning takes time.* A planning team can reduce the workload of individual staff or members.
2. *Planning takes coordination.* A planning team can help integrate and coordinate the planning activities of individual staff.
3. *Planning takes expertise.* A planning team can bring to a particular problem more tools and techniques than any single individual.
4. *Planning takes objectivity.* A planning team can take a broader view than one individual and go beyond specific projects and particular organizational departments.

A planning team generally has three basic areas of responsibility. First, it assists the chief executive in developing goals, strategies, and policies for the organization. The planning group facilitates this process by scanning and monitoring the organization's environment. A second major responsibility of the planning team is to coordinate the planning of different levels and units within the HCO. Finally, the planning group acts as an organizational resource for middle managers, who may lack expertise in planning.

In smaller HCOs, planning and execution must usually be carried out by the same people. Certainly this is a challenge. But the greatest challenge is setting aside time for planning in the midst of all the other activities needed on a day-to-day basis.

RESISTANCE TO THE PLANNING PROCESS

There are three main reasons why planning does not get done in healthcare organizations today: (1) administrators lack training; (2) many perceive planning as irrelevant; and (3) problems can occur in implementation.

Lack of Management Training

Many healthcare organizations are small and utilize a limited managerial force. The educational background and experience of the leaders of these organizations varies widely. Those with prior management experience often possess a proactive, can-do attitude and want to spend their time performing hands-on functions with which they are comfortable. Lost in the press of day-to-day concerns, the objective setting, strategy development, and other planning functions are largely neglected.

Planning Is Thought To Be Irrelevant

Developing objectives and strategies has been largely neglected or purposely avoided by many healthcare organizations. The reluctance to plan stems from the fact that many view the application of strategic planning as irrelevant. Some feel that because the environment in which HCOs work changes so rapidly, laying out formal plans and objectives is a useless endeavor.

With this view, constantly shifting environmental demands outside an HCO's control can make objectives obsolete before they become official doctrine for the organization. So why develop them at all? Unfortunately, the consequence of this perspective is a leadership doomed to reactionary, piecemeal approaches to environmental demands, often resulting in less than desirable performance.

Other strategic goal-setting challenges in HCOs may color attitudes against planning. Most HCOs are service-oriented organizations. Services, unlike products, are intangible and often difficult to separate from the recipient of the service. This complicates specific goal setting and the measurement of results against the goals. In addition, HCOs often employ professionals to deliver their services. Professionals tend to be wed more to their profession and less to the organization's profession and objectives. This is particularly evident when, in the professional's view, the organization's goals conflict with those of their profession.

Finally, HCOs face the daunting task of trying to serve the often varying interests of their clients, service recipients, and funding sponsors. Some might say that setting official goals would serve only to please some constituencies while disaffecting others. However, it is better to be vague than risk losing participation and financial support.

Implementation Problems

Although there is substantial academic and theoretical support for planning, the actual implementation of a plan often runs aground on the shores of operational reality. Even among very progressive healthcare organizations, you find significant resistance to planning. Some of the most common arguments against it are:

1. Planning is not action-oriented.
2. Planning takes too much time; we are too busy to plan.
3. Planning becomes an end, not just a means to an end.
4. Planning never ends up being carried out exactly as intended anyway.

Most of these arguments stem from the same kind of thinking that would say that the pilot was the most important person in the success of an airplane, referring back to the airplane/designer analogy. The feeling that planning is not hands-on and not related to the important day-to-day operations of the HCO is frequently voiced. However, this point of view is shortsighted in terms of long-run success. Planning is not just for dreamers; in fact, it lets the HCO's administrative team determine what can be done today to accomplish or avoid some future circumstance.

Planning sometimes becomes an end in the minds of some users. This is particularly true when established solely as a committee responsibility within an organization. A committee can facilitate the strategic planning process, but the process will not be a dynamic lifeblood activity of the organization without the ongoing involvement of its administrator and staff members.

President Eisenhower has been widely quoted as saying, "Plans are nothing; planning is everything." The truth he expressed was that the actual plan was not the end itself, but that the process of planning–developing futuristic scenarios, evaluating the environment and competition, assessing internal strengths and capabilities, revising objectives and tactics–was the organizational dialogue that was most important. This dialogue ideally breaks down barriers to communication, exposes blind spots to the light of critical scrutiny, tests logic, measures the environment, and determines feasibility. The end result is more effective and efficient implementation of organizational activities.

Planning does not depend on complete forecasting accuracy to be useful. In sports even the very best game plans are often modified as play goes on. Yet coaches continue to develop game plans with each new opponent. They understand that the importance of planning here is to keep your organization moving in the right direction even if the finer points of the plan are constantly being adjusted to new circumstances. And in making these adjustments, a variety of futuristic alternatives or scenarios can be very helpful in establishing planning parameters. Often a best-case, most-likely-case, and worst-case approach is used. This three-level forecast gives dimension to the process of recognizing, anticipating, and "managing" change.

In spite of these and other perceived negatives, the advantages of planning far outweigh any disadvantages. Planning not only should be done but *must* be done.

REVENUE SOURCE INFLUENCES ON PLANNING

Executives of any business enterprise must be concerned about continuing sources of revenue adequate for the survival of their business. Traditional businesses have a straightforward objective. They can focus on pleasing the customer. For the executives of many healthcare organizations, however, revenue concerns are more complex.

For many HCOs, the focus on exactly who the customer is may become fuzzy. This is due to the fact that the recipient of an HCO's services may not be the same person who directly pays the bill. Medicare patients' hospital charges are paid directly by an intervening party, the federal government. The same is true for home healthcare agencies. Public hospitals are largely funded by state legislatures or local municipalities. For many HCOs, services may be funded by donations from individuals and organizations that may never be recipients of the service. Any organization-healthcare-oriented or not-tends to concentrate on the desires of those who foot the bill. And to the extent that there is a funding sponsor providing financial support for the client, the client's influence over the HCO's goals and performance may be weakened.

One consequence of intervening sources of funding for HCOs is the tendency for healthcare organizations to ignore the patient's or client's needs in favor of the funding sponsor's demands where the two conflict. In attempts to satisfy both parties, healthcare organizations may avoid goal setting or develop goals that are vague at best.

Unfortunately, highly generalized goals have their performance shortcomings. In contrast, there is plenty of evidence that goals that are relatively specific and measurable, wherever possible, support higher performance in organizations.

The message for HCOs is that the strategic planning process can provide the understandable goals they need. It does this by systematically considering the expectations of all those who hold a stake in the effectiveness of the HCO's operation. Strategic planning, then, is the vehicle that can produce goals that are defined as clearly as possible toward the end of both meeting the clients' needs and withstanding the scrutiny of the sponsor.

THE GREATEST NEEDS OF TODAY'S HEALTHCARE ORGANIZATIONS

In informal surveys by the authors, leaders of healthcare organizations appear strong in their beliefs that strategic planning is important. Yet simple acknowledgment of its importance is not enough for success. To put matters into perspective, let us try to translate success for your HCO into a formula:

$$X = f(A, B, C, D, E, F, G, H, I \ldots)$$

In this case X represents success, a dependent variable, and is on the left side of the equation. The = sign means a balance, or equal to what is on the other side; the "f" means "a function of," indicating on what that success depends. On the right side are all the independent variables that affect success:

A. Chief Executive as Leader
B. Chief Executive as Manager
C. Planning System
D. Organizational Structure
E. Control System
F. Needs of Constituencies Met
G. HCO Network's National Influence
H. HCO's Local Influence
I. Location
. . . etc.

Only a few independent variables are listed, but the possibilities are endless. Notice that success is not necessarily equated with size. We are defining success in broader terms than number of employees, budget, and so forth. There seems to be a widespread notion that size is the only barometer of success, but we do not subscribe to that belief.

Untapped leadership exists in many HCOs. We believe the greatest problems holding back these leaders-and the organizations they serve-involve some combination of independent variables C, D, and E. Management, planning, organization, and control are some of the greatest needs of HCOs today.

We assume that all HCO administrators are leaders to some degree, or they could not remain in their executive positions. However, their leadership efforts and the success of their organizations are in direct proportion to variables C, D, and E. If you assume all other variables remain unchanged and full effort goes into C, D, and E, then the X factor (success), the dependent variable, has to increase. Without training and knowledge in the area of planning and management, your HCO places a ceiling on success. No organization can get any bigger than the capacity of its managers to manage. The hindrance is not the needs of the constituents, because the needs are always there. Nor is it the HCO's reputation or location; rather, it is simply its management, planning, organization, and control.

If every HCO executive could improve each of these areas just a little each year, they would be much more successful. They could reduce drastically all the obvious errors in direction, false starts, dissipated efforts, staff frustration, and waste. They could also successfully challenge a world rife with criticism about waste and inefficiency in HCOs.

HCO leadership cannot afford to wait until someone comes along and stirs up a big scandal about waste and inefficiency. We need to put our shoulders to the wheel and pay attention to management, planning, organization, control, and people. If we do not, on the whole, many of our healthcare organizations will not accomplish nearly as much as they might.

Our observation is that many people in HCO leadership positions are reluctant to plan, do not want a plan in writing, and do not ask for advice. The tendency is to be led by intuition, which is sometimes based on a whim or emotional impulse. This reflects our general American inclination to "hang loose." Probably 75 percent of the nonhealthcare organizations the authors have observed or worked with have the same problem. Yet the 25 percent that have the discipline to plan and manage properly, far outperform those that do not. Higher revenue surpluses better service, and lower turnover are but a few of the rewards of thoughtful, well-executed planning. Good fortune comes to those HCOs that have the discipline to plan and manage effectively.

Many times there is the tendency to say that forces outside our control caused a plan or project to go sour. And sometimes that is the case. But too often we are our own worst enemies, holding ourselves back. Many HCO failures can be traced to poor planning, failure to get people involved in the planning, and generally poor management.

Even where planning is done, we often sense a spirit of extreme urgency. Here the atmosphere is permeated with a "let's go for it-if it is a worthwhile service, it will prosper" mentality. What is the rush? Many HCOs need to slow down and plan. Often they have rushed around in circles for several years. If our organization provides a worthwhile service, it deserves our best efforts at careful planning. Included in doing our best is using the best planning and management philosophies and techniques available.

Fundamental to these efforts is effective goal setting. The importance of goal setting is to provide direction and unity of purpose. Where planning in HCOs occurs without quantitative goals clearly understood and widely supported, vigorous progress is unlikely and probably impossible. Planning is not easy, but the alternative is for the organization to be tossed to and fro, buffeted by every unforeseen circumstance, and blown off course.

And on a personal level, every leader needs a vision or a dream. Mission statements and dreams are the vessels through which personal desires can be fulfilled. Yet without specific goals, a vision is no vision.

In a society where many institutions are becoming stagnant, it is imperative that HCOs have an expanding vision. Thus, we see creative planning as the healthcare organization's best hope for a successful future. Solid purpose, long-range dreaming, and visionary thinking should be basic to an HCO's operation. Too often planning in HCOs has been met with little enthusiasm. Even in larger organizations, the enthusiasm for a plan seldom extends beyond a year unless it involves something tangible, such as a new building. Yet no matter how misunderstood and poorly appreciated planning is, it is a major factor in effective HCO performance. The time for strategic planning in your healthcare organization is *now.*

SUMMARY

We have attempted to establish in this chapter our belief that: (1) the demands of a volatile environment for HCOs support, overall, a growing urgency for the planning concept; (2) many of the identifiable HCO failures cannot be blamed solely on unforeseen and uncontrollable factors; yet (3) many leaders do not believe that there is a need for planning; but (4) there is a critical place for better planning and management; and last, (5) methods used successfully in industry are applicable to healthcare organizations.

The philosophy of this book is that in order for everyone in a healthcare organization–the Board, the executive staff, the employees–to be successful, a strategic plan is desperately needed. If you look at the mistakes of the past, it is obvious that many HCOs have floundered because they lack strategic direction. Over years of consulting with these types of organizations, the authors have observed this exact pattern in a large number of them. However, if you take the time and effort to study this book, apply the format prescribed here, and follow up with your people, this is what we believe you can expect:

1. A sense of enthusiasm in your organization.
2. A five-year plan in writing to which everyone is committed.
3. A sense of commitment by the entire organization to its overall direction.
4. Clear job duties and responsibilities.
5. Time for the leaders to do what they need to do.
6. Clear and evident improvement in the health and vitality of every member of the organization's staff.
7. Measurable improvement in the personal lives of all those in management positions with time for vacations, family, and personal pursuits.

8. The ability to measure very specifically the growth and contributions made by executives at the close of their careers.
9. More effective leadership of the healthcare organization because a plan is in place in writing and is understood–even more important, a management team and philosophy will be in place to guide the organization into its next era of growth.

In this chapter we have presented our belief that implementing strategic management in healthcare organizations can provide more effective performance, a belief that has gained much ground in the last decade. Vast social questions and complex conditions in almost every community now demand the need for good management in these organizations.

The next chapter presents an overview of the entire strategic planning process. Then the following chapters cover each step of the planning process. The theory behind each step is presented, and actual examples are given to help understand that step. Make notes on your own situation as you read. Appendix A consolidates the worksheets found at the end of each chapter to prepare your strategic plan, and also displays an outline for presenting it. Read on with excitement!

REFERENCES

1. Cerne, Frank. "The Winners! Taking Charge of Their Destinies," *Hospitals & Health Networks* (July 20, 1994), pp. 25-31.

2. Taravella, Steve. "UniHealth in Fast Lane After Making Merger," *Modern Healthcare* (June 11, 1990), pp. 59-65.

3. Cerne, Frank. "The Winners! Taking Charge of Their Destinies," *Hospitals & Health Networks* (July 20, 1994), pp. 25-31.

4. Greene, Jay. "Hospitals Can Boost Profits by Going According to Plan," *Modern Healthcare* (August 5, 1991), p. 36.

5. Hammonds, Keith H. "The Administrator," *Business Week* (January 17, 1994), p. 61.

6. Fottler, Myron D. "Health Care Organizational Performance: Present and Future Research," *Journal of Management* (Vol. 13, No. 2), pp. 367-391.

7. Jauch, Larry R., and W. F. Glueck. *Strategic Management and Business Policy.* New York: McGraw-Hill, 1988, p. 32.

8. "1993-A Boom Year for Healthcare Mergers and Acquisitions." *Modern Healthcare* 23, No. 48, 1993, p. 6.

9. Fottler, Myron D. "Is Management Really Generic?" *Academy of Management Review* (January 1981), p. 2.

Chapter 2

Overview of Strategic Planning

"Cheshire Puss," she [Alice] began . . . "Would you please tell me which way I ought to go from here?"
"That depends on where you want to get to," said the cat.

Lewis Carroll
Alice in Wonderland

This chapter presents an overview of the strategic planning process. Each of the areas that are discussed in this chapter is dealt with in more detail in later chapters. The intention here is to provide an introduction to the major components of the process.

WHAT IS STRATEGIC PLANNING?

The word "strategic" means "pertaining to strategy." Strategy is derived from the Greek word *strategos,* which means "generalship," "art of the general," or, more broadly, "leadership." The word "strategic" when used in the context of planning provides a perspective to planning that is long-run in nature and deals with achieving specified end results. Just as military strategy has as its objective the winning of the war, so, too, strategic planning has as its goal the achievement of your organization's purpose–service to your clients.

Strategic decisions must be differentiated from tactical decisions. Strategic decisions outline the overall game plan or approach, while tactical decisions involve implementing various activities that are needed to carry out the larger strategy. For example, a service organization that decides to change locations because of shifting population trends and industrial development around the present location is making strategic decisions. Then many other decisions must be made about exact location, size of the building, parking facilities, and other major details. These all have long-term implications and are therefore strategic in nature.

Then other decisions, such as those pertaining to wall colors, decor, and air-conditioning, must be made. These are tactical decisions needed to carry out or implement the strategic decision previously made. Thus, strategic decisions provide the overall framework within which the tactical decisions are made. It is critically important that leaders of healthcare organizations be able to differentiate between these types of decisions to identify whether the decision has short-term or long-term implications.

THE STRATEGIC PLANNING PROCESS

The strategic planning process is basically a matching process involving an HCO's internal resources and its external opportunities. The objective of this process is to peer through the "strategic window" and identify opportunities that the individual organization is equipped to take advantage of or respond to. Thus the strategic planning process can be defined as *a managerial process that involves matching the healthcare organization's capabilities with its opportunities.* These opportunities are identified over time and decisions revolve around investing or divesting resources to address these opportunities. The contexts in which these strategic decisions are made are: (1) the HCO's operating environment; (2) the HCO's purpose or mission; and (3) the HCO's organization-wide objectives. Strategic planning is the process that ties all these elements together to facilitate strategic choices that are consistent with all three areas and then implements and evaluates these choices. Appendix A presents an outline of a strategic plan. The successful results of planning described earlier can be achieved through implementing an effective strategic planning process. The following breakdown of this process is a complete outline of a system capable of creating true change in your healthcare organization's attitudes as well as in its productivity.

It is important to recognize at this point what we call "the two Ps." The first "P" means Product: get the plan in writing. The plan must be something you can hold in your hand, a written product of your efforts. If the plan is not in writing, it is simply daydreaming. When it is in writing, you are telling yourself and others you are serious about it. The second "P" represents Process: every plan must have maximum input from everyone. Those who execute the plan must be involved in construction of the plan in order to gain their commitment. The best way to ensure a plan's failure is to overlook both the product and the process. They are equally important.

While there are many different ways in which an HCO can approach the strategic planning process, a systematic approach that carries the organization through a series of integral steps helps focus attention on answering a basic set of questions each organization must answer:

1. *What will we do?* This question focuses attention on the specific needs the HCO will try to meet.
2. *Who will we do it for?* This question addresses the need for an HCO to identify the various groups whose needs will be met.
3. *How will we do what we want to do?* Answering this question forces thinking about the many avenues through which an HCO's efforts may be channeled.

The strategic planning process used by an organization must force the HCO's leadership to deal with these questions on a continuous basis. Ongoing answers to these most fundamental questions allow the organization to continuously adapt over time and do the work it is best suited to do.

Strategic planning is defined as a process that involves completing the following steps:

1. Defining an organization's purpose and reason for being.
2. Analyzing environmental opportunities and threats, assessing the HCO's own strengths and weaknesses, and making assumptions about future operating conditions.
3. Prescribing written, specific, and measurable objectives in the principal result areas that contribute to the organization's purpose.

4. Developing strategies on how to use available resources to meet objectives.
5. Developing operational plans to meet objectives, including plans for all individuals in the organization.
6. Setting up control and evaluation procedures to determine if performance is keeping pace with attainment of objectives and if it is consistent with defined purpose.

The six steps of the strategic planning process are illustrated in Exhibit 2.1. They are important because they force the organization to consider certain questions. As each step requires the people at various organizational levels to discuss, study, and negotiate, the process as a whole fosters a planning mentality. When the six steps are complete, the end result is a strategic plan for the organization, specifying why the organization exists, what it is trying to accomplish, and how resources will be utilized to accomplish objectives

Exhibit 2.1. The Strategic Planning Process

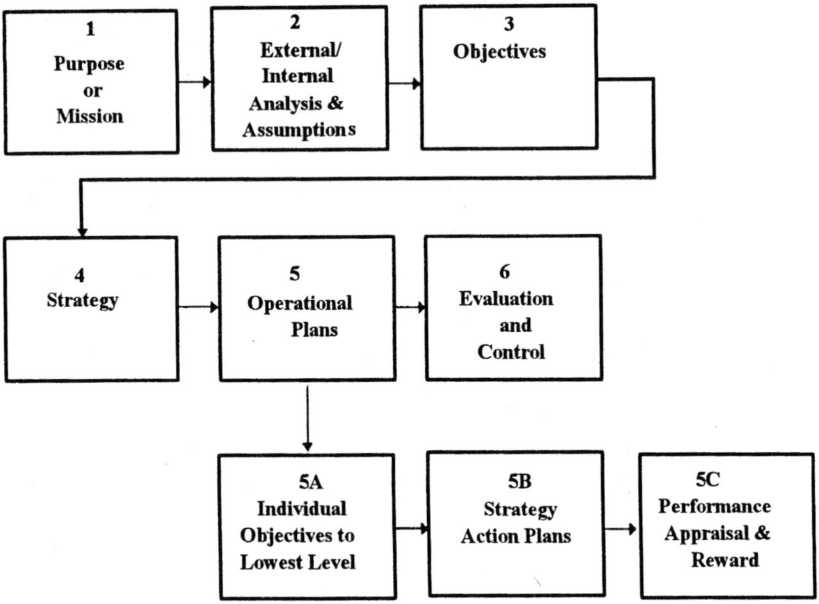

and fulfill its purpose. Let us briefly describe each of the six planning stages.

Defining Purpose

The first and probably the most important consideration when developing a strategic plan is to define the purpose, mission, or "reason for being" for the organization as a whole. Subsequently, in support of this umbrella mission statement, statements of purpose should also be written for specific divisions of organizations of size.

Writing the statement of purpose is usually a difficult process, even though it may appear simple. Multiple, often diverse views of the HCO's fundamental purpose may exist because of the differing perspectives of the numerous constituencies that hold a stake in the performance of the organization. Nevertheless, as Peter Drucker, noted management authority, emphasizes, "The best nonprofits devote a great deal of thought to defining their organization's mission."[1] Certainly this would be true of proprietary HCOs as well.

For example, an inner-city hospital that defines itself as "a delivery system for the healthcare of the needy" may be on the right track but will constantly face the need to explain and expand this definition. Does "healthcare" mean only acute inpatient care or does it include other services, such as neighborhood clinics? If other services are added to the definition, will they involve only traditional physical care or will they address other needs, such as psychological counseling or substance abuse treatment? Granted, these things may change as the organization evolves and grows; but thinking through these issues provides a sense of vision and also avoids going off on tangential activities that do not fit with what the organization wants to do or be.

The purpose statement should present the dream and vision of what the organization aspires to be. This should be a participative process. Each of the success stories noted in Chapter 1 had this participative nature in common.

Organizational members should try to visualize what they want the organization to become. If the participants can see where they are going and have an image of the real mission of the organization, plans will fall into place more easily. The critical implementation phase of the plan will go more smoothly as the participants buy into the process and make it their own.

A vision of what can be accomplished creates the spark and energy for the whole planning and management process. It is important to spend ample time defining this purpose statement. The process should emphasize getting everyone involved in the dream of how things can be. Without a vision, people just work day-to-day and tend not to be as productive or willing to go all out as they could be.

In addition, a good statement of purpose not only clarifies what the HCO does, it sets boundaries. It defines what the organization will not do. It helps limit expectations, and that alone can make it the HCO administrator's best friend.

Analysis and Assumptions

It is vital for your HCO to gauge the environment within which it operates. This should be standard practice for all HCOs. The only way we can manage change is to constantly monitor the environment within which we operate. This analysis stage is where we look at the environment external to our organization for potential threats and opportunities and compare them against our internal operation for strengths and weaknesses.

For example, some "downtown" hospitals faced the dilemma of whether to remain in the downtown area or move to the suburbs. In these instances, the HCOs found that their historic location resulted in two significant problems: lack of space to grow and changes in the socioeconomic makeup of the neighborhood. The socioeconomic changes made the organization less effective in meeting the needs of those in the neighborhood who were less able to afford healthcare services. Potential patients with greater ability to afford care had moved and now sought care closer to their new homes.

Their solution was quite interesting. They bought land and built satellite hospitals in growing parts of their community. Everybody won! The old neighborhood hospitals could serve the needs of those who lived there, while the new hospitals were built in areas where they could grow and help fund care at the inner-city facilities.

Many organizations have found it useful to use an analytical framework referred to earlier as a SWOT analysis. SWOT is an acronym for *s*trengths, *w*eaknesses, *o*pportunities, and *t*hreats.

Strengths and weaknesses refer to elements internal to the organization, while opportunities and threats are external to the organization. A detailed SWOT analysis helps the HCO take a good look at the organization's favorable and unfavorable factors with a view toward building on strengths and eliminating or minimizing weaknesses. At the same time, the HCO's leadership must also assess external opportunities that could be pursued and threats that must be dealt with in order to survive.

The next stage is to state your major assumptions. These should be made about situations over which you have little or absolutely no control, such as the external environment. One good place to start is to extend some of the items studied in the external analysis. Should this stage appear relatively unimportant in developing a strategic plan, consider this: by not making explicit assumptions, you are making one major implicit assumption–things are going to remain the same and nothing that happens is important enough to affect you. An extraordinarily dangerous assumption these days!

Establishing Objectives

Often the words "key results," "goals," and "targets" are used synonymously with objectives when thinking about long- and short-term objectives. Think of an archer drawing an arrow and aiming directly at a target. The bull's-eye represents exactly where you want to be at a certain point in time. You want all of your organization's arrows aimed at the same target. An archer who shoots arrows off in any direction is liable to hit almost anything–including the wrong target. People get confused and disorganized if they do not know where they are going.

Objectives must be clear, concise, written statements outlining what is to be accomplished in key priority areas over a certain time period. Wherever possible, they should be expressed in measurable terms that are consistent with the overall purpose of the organization.

Objectives are the results desired upon completion of the period the plan covers. In the absence of objectives, no sense of direction can be attained in decision making. A basic truism is: "If you don't know where you are going, any road will get you there." In planning, objectives answer one of the basic questions posed in the planning process: where do we want to go? These objectives become the focal point for strategy decisions.

Another basic purpose served by objectives is in the evaluation of performance. Objectives in the strategic plan become the yardsticks used to evaluate performance. As will be pointed out later, it is impossible to evaluate performance without some standard against which results can be measured. The objectives become the standards for evaluating performance because they are the statement of results desired by the planner.

Strategy Development

After developing a set of objectives for the time period covered by the strategic plan, the methods or strategy needed to accomplish those objectives must be formulated. This is accomplished in stages.

First, strategy alternatives must be developed and alternative courses of action evaluated by management before commitment is made to a specific option. From these, an overall strategy can be designed. Then operational strategies for each major service area can be developed to detail activities to accomplish the grand strategy. In so doing, strategy becomes the link between objectives and results.

Operational Plans

After these steps have been taken and a strategy has been developed to meet your objectives and goals, it is time to develop operational or action plans. The operational plan stage is the "action" or "doing" stage. Here you hire, fire, build, advertise, and so on. How many times has a group of people planned something, gotten enthusiastic–and nothing happened? This is usually because they did not complete an operational or action plan to implement their strategy.

Operational plans need to be developed in all the areas that are used to support the overall strategy. These include service delivery operations, information systems, finance, marketing, and human resources. Each of these more detailed plans is designed to spell out what needs to happen in a given area to implement the strategic plan.

Supporting the operational plans are the individual plans of all members of the organization. These are shown as steps 5A, 5B, and

5C in Exhibit 2.1. When planning is carried from the top to the lowest level in the organization, everyone becomes involved in negotiating and setting personal performance objectives that support the organization's objectives. Then individuals begin to develop their own action plans, which are used to accomplish these objectives. Finally, performance appraisals, which must be done on an individual basis, use those personal performance objectives as the basis of appraisal and reward.

Evaluation and Control

Failure to establish procedures to appraise and control the strategic plan can lead to less than optimal performance. A plan is not complete until the controls are identified and the procedures for recording and transmitting control information to the administrators of the plan are established. Many organizations fail to understand the importance of establishing procedures to appraise and control the planning process. Control should be a natural follow-through in developing a plan.

Planning and control should be integral processes. The strategic planning process results in a strategic plan. This plan is implemented (activities are performed in the manner described in the plan), and results are produced. These results may be reflected in services rendered, financial sponsorship, volunteer participation, and image enhancement.

Information on these and other key result areas can be used by HCO executives to compare the results with original objectives to evaluate performance. This performance evaluation identifies the areas where decisions must be made to adjust activities, people, or finances. The actual decision making controls the plan by altering it to accomplish stated objectives, and a new cycle begins.

Individual performance appraisal is a vital part of this step. Rewards or reprimands must be related to the personal achievement or lack of achievement of agreed-upon objectives. This creates a work environment where people know what to do and rewards are tied to performance.

STRATEGIC PLANNING AS AN ONGOING PROCESS

Strategic planning is not simply a singular event to be repeated only every three to five years. The word "process" can be defined as a series of actions or operations leading to an end. Here, we wish to emphasize the ongoing action aspect of the planning process. The actions are the activities in which the HCO engages to accomplish objectives and fulfill its mission. In today's dynamic environments, these activities must continually evolve.

There are several important reasons for viewing strategic planning as a process. First is the idea that a process can be studied and improved. An HCO just getting involved in strategic planning will need to review the whole process on an annual basis, not only to account for changing environmental forces but to improve or refine the plan. Purpose statements, objectives, strategies, and appraisal techniques can be fine-tuned over time as the planners gain more experience and as new and better information becomes available.

A second reason for viewing strategic planning as a process is that a change in any component of the process will affect most or all of the other components. For example, a change in purpose or objective will lead to new analysis, strategies, and evaluations. Thus, major changes that affect the organization must lead to a reevaluation of all the elements of the plan.

Finally, and perhaps most important, involvement in the strategic planning process can become the vehicle through which the whole organization mobilizes its energies to accomplish its purpose. If all members of the organization can participate in the process in some way, an atmosphere can be created within the organization that implies that doing the right things and doing things right is everybody's job. Participation instills ownership. It's not "my plan" or "their plan" but "our plan" that becomes important, and everyone will *want* to make a contribution to make it happen.

STRATEGY IMPLEMENTATION

The focus of this book is on the strategic planning process, which results in the development of a strategic plan. This plan becomes the blueprint for carrying out the many activities in which an HCO is involved. There are many other issues that determine the effectiveness of an organization that are beyond the scope of this book. These issues essentially revolve around implementing the strategic plan through: (1) staffing and training personnel and other constituents, (2) developing organizational relationships among staff and constituents, (3) achieving commitment, (4) developing a positive organizational culture, (5) leadership styles, and (6) personnel evaluation and reward systems.

Our lack of discussion of these topics is due to space limitation and a desire to keep the length of the book manageable for readers. Both effective planning and implementation are needed to create an effective organization. The strategic plan concentrates on "doing the right things" while implementation concentrates on "doing things right." Examples of several entire strategic plans for HCOs are presented in Appendix B.

SUMMARY

This chapter has presented an overview of the strategic planning process, in which a series of thought-provoking questions must be answered. The process is a set of integral steps that carries the planners through a sequence that involves providing answers to these questions and then continually rethinking and reevaluating these answers as the organization and its environment change.

A helpful tool to use at this stage is the Planning Process Worksheet located at the end of this chapter and in Appendix A. This form, when thoughtfully filled out, will provide an assessment of your current position in terms of planning and management of your organization. It will help point out where to direct your efforts as you work to improve the efficiency and effectiveness of the organization entrusted to your leadership.

REFERENCE

1. Drucker, P. F. "What Business Can Learn From Non-Profits," *Harvard Business Review* (July-August, 1989), p. 89.

PLANNING PROCESS WORKSHEET

This worksheet is provided to aid your healthcare organization in starting the strategic planning process. Use the answers to these questions to provide a foundation for completing the remaining worksheets.

1. Who should be involved in the planning process?

___

___

___

2. Where will planning sessions be held?

___

___

___

3. When will planning sessions be held?

___

___

___

4. What types of background material do participants need prior to starting the first session?

___

___

___

5. Who will lead the process? Who will ultimately be responsible for arranging sessions, and getting material typed, reproduced, and distributed?

___

___

___

6. When and how will the staff, board, employees, or others be involved in the process?

____

____

____

7. How will the results be communicated to everyone in the organization?

____

____

____

8. Who will train/supervise managers in working with their own staff and in setting objectives, developing action plans, and conducting performance appraisals?

____

____

____

9. How frequently will the process be reviewed and by whom?

____

____

____

10. Who will be responsible for dealing with external groups (revenue sources, independent healthcare professionals, media, consultants) in preparing the plan?

____

____

____

Chapter 3

Defining Organizational Purpose

Where there is no vision, the people perish.

Solomon
Proverbs 29:18

However brilliant an action may be, it should not be accounted great when it is not the result of a great purpose.

François de La Rochefoucauld

No enterprise can exist for itself alone. It ministers to some need, it performs some great service not for itself but for others; or failing therein it ceases to be profitable and ceases to exist.

Calvin Coolidge

This chapter outlines the first step in the strategic planning process: defining your purpose or mission. Without a clear and carefully considered statement of purpose, all other stages of the process will be misguided. Accordingly, we will discuss the value of defining the healthcare organization's purpose, describe how to write effective mission statements, and present examples of mission statements.

THE IMPORTANCE OF DEFINING PURPOSE

The first and probably most important consideration when developing a strategic plan is to define the purpose, mission, or "reason for being" of the organization or any specific part of it. This is usually a difficult process. Recall the successful turnarounds of Mercy Health System and Holy Cross Hospital discussed in Chapter 1. Even in the midst of their respective crisis situations, both institutions rethought their missions as the fundamental step in moving toward greater institutional effectiveness.

Peter Drucker, management consultant and writer, has led the way in stressing the importance of defining purpose. Drucker notes the importance of identifying an organization's purpose by emphasizing that it is the process of organizing to satisfy a need in the marketplace. The mission concept should be client-oriented in that it should be defined by the want the customer satisfies when buying a product or a service. Before profit or financial success, satisfying the customer is the mission and purpose of every business.[1]

Organizations need a clear definition of purpose and mission because that is the only way to obtain clear and realistic business objectives. It is the foundation for priorities, strategies, plans, and work assignments. The mission is the starting point for the design of managerial structure and jobs.[2]

Clearly, if purpose is defined casually or introspectively, the basis for how an organization goes about achieving its objectives rests on shaky foundations. If we do not know what we are about, then anything we do, regardless of its true effectiveness, can be made to sound as if it were the best course of action. This can be self-deluding and self-defeating, taking us away from the long-run basis for our existence: meeting customers' needs.

It is not always easy to formulate a statement of purpose. The purpose statement should embody the dream and vision of what the organization wants to be. Members should try to visualize what they want the organization to be. If they can see where they are going and have an image of the real mission of the organization, the implementation of their plans will fall more easily into place.

It is important to understand this concept of purpose and vision in order to have a successful HCO operation. The vision is what unites your staff and spurs them to higher performance. Without a long-term perspective, an HCO will continually swerve off course instead of moving with steadiness and certainty toward its goals.

It is in the purpose statement that the vision and the dream for the HCO must be reflected. This purpose statement sets the stage for all planning. A clear mission statement provides a starting point for determining goals and objectives as specific measures of mission effectiveness.

Objectives, which are covered later in the text, must by their very nature contribute to achieving what is in the purpose statement. Without objectives, a mission statement becomes an empty platitude. Too often this link is missed. For example, in a study of private Christian college and university administrations, it was discovered that all those surveyed had a purpose and mission statement, but only 50 percent had specific measurable objectives of what was to be accomplished.

In summary, six reasons may be suggested for a healthcare organization to have a mission statement:

1. It provides a reason for being, an explanation to ourselves and others as to why we exist as an organization.
2. It sets boundaries around our operations and thus defines what we will do and what we will not do.
3. It describes the need we are attempting to meet in the world and how we are going to respond to that need.
4. It acts as the foundation on which the primary objectives of the organization can be based.
5. It helps to form the basis for the ethos or culture (that is, the guiding beliefs and underlying values) of the organization.
6. It helps us to communicate to those outside the organization what we are all about.

BASIC ELEMENTS OF AN EFFECTIVE MISSION STATEMENT

In developing a mission statement, several basic elements should be reflected:

1. *History.* Every organization has a history that includes past problems, accomplishments, objectives, and policies. The mission statement should reflect the historical significance of such characteristics.

2. *Distinctive competencies.* This element reflects what the organization is uniquely equipped to do because of its location, personnel, resources, or historical position. While most organizations can do many things, they can do some things so well that they have an advantage over other organizations in certain areas.

3. *Needs, segments, and technology.* The mission statement must reflect what we will do (needs met or values received by clients), who we will do it for (patient/client groups or segments to be served, since we can't be all things to all people), and what technology will be used (how needs will be met).

4. *Environment.* Each organization operates in an environment that dictates the opportunities and threats that must be dealt with when a mission statement is developed. Laws structuring insurance policies, and fear of diseases transmitted, are examples of environmental factors that influence an organization's ability to achieve its purpose.

Using the above four perspectives, ultimately we seek to answer in our mission statement three basic questions about the nature of our enterprise:

1. What kind of organization are we? In other words, what services or methods of service delivery do we offer that make us unique among our competitors?
2. What kind of organization do we want to be? This deals with our vision of what we aspire to be as a service provider as opposed to what we currently do. For many organizations, this distinction is important because there is often a performance gap between what we actually do and who we truly are versus our view of what we hope to become and eventually accomplish.
3. What kind of organization should we be? This final question is perhaps the most important of the three when we consider the possibility that what we are and what we hope to be could both be wrong. In changing environments, who we are and what we do must continually adapt in order to achieve continued organizational vitality.

It is not unusual for an organization to work on a mission statement for months or even years before deciding that it really reflects what the organization wants to become. Once developed, the mission statement is not a once-and-forever document. As the HCO adapts itself to the demands of a changing environment, so should the mission statement reflect this adaptation. It must be reviewed periodically and updated as appropriate to continually reflect the HCO's fundamental purposes. This is a difficult and thought-provoking process when approached correctly, but it must be done. As stated earlier, what an organization does (objectives and strategies) should flow from what the organization is (mission or purpose).

WRITING A STATEMENT OF PURPOSE

The following set of guidelines offers helpful tips on writing and evaluating a purpose statement.

Determine Your Fundamental Reason for Being

For an HCO under development, this means expressly determining what need satisfaction you will offer your clients. If your HCO is currently operating and not a new start-up, this means moving your thinking beyond simply what you now do. You must specifically identify what the need satisfaction *should* be for your HCO. Identifying your basic purpose for existence also means wrestling with what need satisfaction your HCO may be offering in the future.

One outcome of these considerations should be a section of the statement that is specific enough to offer guidance to the HCO's staff in the near term. But there should also be a general aspect that looks to the future and provides "stretching room" for your HCO to adapt and grow with future needs. Done effectively, these aspects of the mission statement serve as a touchstone, reminding the HCO staff why they do what they do.

Identify Your Principal Methods for Delivering Need Satisfaction

This issue focuses on the basic activities and functions your HCO will employ to meet the needs of your clientele. Verbs are the key here. "Produce," "provide," "market," "offer," and "serve" are all action words representative of basic delivery activities. Here, the HCO must deal with the issue of to what extent it will develop products or services in-house as opposed to acquiring them from outside sources and then coordinating their delivery in a way that provides value to the client.

Determine the Scope of Your Mission

This involves determining whom you intend to serve. Proper deliberation here focuses attention outside the nuts and bolts of internal activities. It forces consideration of the intended recipients of your HCO's functions. At a practical level, scope identifies the breadth of delivery–local neighborhood, community-wide, regional, national, or international. If your operation is part of a larger organization, the parent organization becomes part of your clientele served, since your mission should support the parent organization's purpose on the one hand and be accountable to it on the other. In effect, you are writing a mission for your unit that delivers on the larger organization's purpose for a constituency that is smaller than that of the parent organization. For instance, a large hospital chain has a mission that seeks to serve an entire nation. But a local hospital within the network should define its mission in terms of applying the national purpose to a specific constituency, such as the local community.

Determine That Portion of the Above Mission Statement for Which Your Unit Is Accountable

While the national chain's mission might include many services, such as managed care, help in ending chemical dependency, and psychiatric care, a local hospital's capabilities within the chain may be more limited, focusing on traditional acute care services. Your mission statement should reflect these differences where they exist.

Prepare a Rough Draft of the Mission Statement That Covers the Purpose of the Group and the Major Activities It Performs

With a working team, such as the administrative staff and board of directors, a rough-draft mission statement can be developed at an all-day meeting, using an outside facilitator who is familiar with communications techniques, group processes, and the concept of mission statements. The meeting can begin with each individual jotting down his or her own version of the mission statement. When these drafts are all assembled, the group can review each one for clarity and understanding. Finally, combine those portions that are similar, so that only areas of wide disagreement are left. At this point, negotiations can be carried out among members of the group until there is general agreement on all points ("I am able to live with this"). The final result is the rough draft of the mission statement.

SAMPLE MISSION STATEMENTS

It might be helpful at this point to examine some mission statements prepared by various healthcare organizations. Note that, while these statements vary in their comprehensiveness, they all attempt to reflect the uniqueness of the organizations in terms of their reason for being and also serve as guidelines for what the organization should be doing. These statements were developed through a process involving many people. Initial statements were revised many times to add specificity and clarity to the terms used to define purpose.

A Large, Multiple-Hospital Consortium

Purpose and Mission. A working partnership committed to improving the health status of people in our communities. The alliance exists to help partners and their allies succeed in carrying out this commitment by: providing sustained leadership for the positive transformation of health services organization and delivery; transferring knowledge and experience relating to health services delivery, and developing new methods and knowledge; supporting the linkage of efforts and integration of services in networks, so as to serve communities better; and providing cost-effective resources for the improvement of health status.[3]

A Large, Metropolitan, Not-for-Profit Hospital

To provide medical and hospital services for the sick and disabled of any race, creed, color, or nationality, and to carry on such educational, philanthropic, and scientific activities and functions as are a part of efficient, modern hospital service.

A Small, Rural, Not-for-Profit Hospital

We exist to create an environment where healing can occur and wellness is promoted.

A Nursing Home (Single Facility)

Our team of professionals' fundamental purpose is to provide an atmosphere of caring that will deliver health and well-being to all its constituents.[4]

A Nursing Home Chain

Our purpose is to improve your health so that you can return home.[5]

A Home Healthcare Agency

Our mission is for clients and their families, to offer a wide range of services designed to keep the client in the comfort of his/her own home while decreasing the stress on family members and/or significant others; for referral sources and contracts, to offer convenient one-stop shopping to referral sources and contracts that include: (1) speedy response time, (2) high-quality care, (3) customer satisfaction, (4) a wide range of services, (5) competitive pricing; and for our employees, to offer a mentally healthy environment where employees are encouraged to grow and develop their talents.[6]

A Regional Office of the Department of Veterans Affairs

Our mission is to administer benefits to veterans and their families and provide quality services to our customers in a timely, compassionate manner. Our vision is to be recognized as the finest provider of benefits and quality service in Veterans Affairs–always striving to achieve a higher level of excellence and to earn the trust and respect of veterans, their families, and other customers, in a diverse environment that cultivates the full participation of all our employees.[7]

A Community Health Center

The primary mission of the Center is to provide quality community based family health and medical services. Our goals are "To Be the Best We Can Be" and to provide patient satisfaction in all aspects of our service. The Center is in the business of caring–caring for our patients, caring for our communities, and caring for our staff. We provide care for individuals of all ages and incomes, regardless of ability to pay, who reside in the southeastern part of our state. Services provided are carried out in a friendly, prompt, cost-effective, and caring manner.

The Center is an organization which values its communities, its employees, and its patients. The Center supports an environment for professional growth and development, based on shared values of its community, Board members, and staff toward the delivery of community healthcare.

The Center offers a range of primary health and medical care services, including health education, social services, transportation, and information services, which support the philosophy of keeping the person as independent and close to home as practical and clinically indicated. Practitioners provide continuity of care from outpatient through inpatient hospital follow-up, and social and nutritional services.

The Center is committed to continuing high standards of service delivered in a cost-effective manner. This requires the maintenance of financial integrity and appropriate utilization of resources.

The Center plays a leadership role in addressing and responding to state, regional, local health and related needs. The foundation and orientation of the Center comes from strong relationships with the communities it serves. This includes policy setting by community members of the Board of Directors, Advisory Committee input and support, and responsiveness to the needs of our patients and users of all programs.[8]

A Drug Abuse Program

The mission of the Drug Abuse Program is to provide free support and counseling to young people, families, and communities of the city, county, and surrounding area who are experiencing hardships and problems related to drug and alcohol abuse.

We, the Board of Trustees, staff, and volunteers of the program, pledge to actively seek the fulfillment of this mission and in order to do so will seek to:

- Provide viable and effective solutions to young people and families suffering from the effects of drug and alcohol abuse.
- Offer informational and educational services that are of the highest quality.
- Provide and/or promote sound prevention models that address area youth, families, and communities.

We also understand that, undertaking this task, we assume the additional responsibility of protecting/preserving the effectiveness and good name now historically associated with the Drug Abuse Program. In doing so, the program's traditions and means of operating should always be considered, so that objectives in meeting the mission statement do not conflict with already proven success. Be it not mistaken, this endeavor is of selfless motivation and is hereby dedicated to the health of our young people and to their families.

The American Heart Association

The mission of the American Heart Association is to reduce death and disability due to cardiovascular disease and stroke.

A Recreation Center for the Physically Limited

The goal of this corporation is to enable persons over the age of five with physical disabilities in the metropolitan area to enhance their lives. To this end, we offer opportunities for growth and self-fulfillment in a recreational setting.

In recognition of the fact that this commitment to the quest for a fuller life by persons with physical disabilities cannot be met solely within the confines of our program or facility, we additionally recognize our responsibility for becoming aware of and addressing the issues important to persons with physical disabilities within the community as a whole. To accomplish this aim, while concentrating on our primary program of growth through recreation, we will seek to participate in cooperative efforts with other groups and agencies actually and potentially representing and/or serving citizens with physical disabilities.

A Regional Arthritis Foundation Chapter

The mission of this regional Arthritis Foundation chapter is to provide information and education about arthritis and related diseases, as well as chapter programs and services; to provide an appropriate range of quality services to those individuals and families affected by these diseases; and to work with professionals involved in the diagnosis and treatment of arthritis-related diseases through the provision of education, information, and funding of research. In order to accomplish this mission and to support the efforts of the National Arthritis Foundation, the chapter actively solicits contributions of time, resources, and financial support.

Area Council on Alcoholism and Drug Abuse

The Area Council on Alcoholism and Drug Abuse is an education and information agency providing health and wellness programs that helps build capable, responsible, independent people, thereby reducing the risk and the incidence of the dependencies of alcoholism or other drug abuse. The goal of ACADA is to help each client develop healthy perceptions and the skills that produce capabilities of self-confidence, judgment, responsibility, and self-esteem, and therein increase his/her capacity to love and care for themselves.

In summary, a purpose statement needs to be built around several points. The first of these involves internal operations and functions. Typically this includes a description of the fundamental activities the HCO engages in, specifically, the basic services provided, such as inpatient acute care, outreach clinics, managed care systems, wellness programs, health education and training, and so on. This aspect of the statement thus answers the "what do we do?" question.

A second area that should be reflected in the purpose statement is external clientele. This part of the statement focuses on identifying the customers/clients/patients to be served by the HCO. This may include descriptions of demographic characteristics (such as the needy or the homeless) as well as geographic boundaries (such as the Dallas, Texas, metropolitan area). This portion of the statement emphasizes answers to the "who do we serve?" question.

A final area that should be addressed is needs served. The emphasis here is on the needs of constituencies that will be met. These are the ultimate ends we hope to achieve, such as better preventive healthcare, more comprehensive acute care services, improved access to healthcare services for the region, and so on. This section identifies who we are and hope to be, giving our staff an identity to hold on to in uncertain times and the leeway to stretch toward new services and greater goal attainment of existing ones.

We have chosen to include a number of actual mission statements to demonstrate variety in actual practice. The reader can see that many do not contain all the elements we are arguing for. However, for an example of a fairly comprehensive statement, please look back at the mission statement of the drug abuse program. Note how the detail in this mission statement identifies what is to be done and for whom it is to be done. The references to prevention, education, and problem solving related to drug abuse identify key success areas for the development of objectives and strategies. Target clientele are also specified in the statement–young people and their families.

A final thought here. What should be avoided in mission statements is an overly philosophical tone that, in essence, says, "We are going to do something good for someone out there somewhere." A mission statement should create a distinct sense of unity and purpose. If it is too general and all-encompassing, it is not meaningfully actionable–the ultimate purpose of a purpose statement.

EVALUATING A PURPOSE STATEMENT

The list below can be used as a guide to evaluate a statement of purpose. The idea is to come up with a statement that really represents what the organization wants to be or should be to survive.

1. Broadness and continuity of application – the statement should be broad enough to cover all significant areas of activity expected of the organization without a specific termination period indicated.
2. Functional commitment – the nature of the works, tasks, or activities to be performed must be defined in terms that will determine clearly the validity of the group or organization.
3. Resource commitment – the statement should include a commitment to cost-effective utilization of available resources.
4. Unique or distinctive nature of work – every unit in an organization should make some unique or distinctive contribution. If there are two or more units in an organization with identical mission statements, the risk of duplicated effort is obvious.
5. Description of services to be offered.
6. Description of group or groups to be served.
7. Geographical area to be covered.

Sometimes it is useful to use a series of questions to evaluate a purpose statement after it is written. A "no" answer to one of the questions means the statement needs to be reworded to more clearly reflect the organization's basic reason for being. The following list of questions may be useful to you:

1. Does it contain all important commitments?
2. Does it clearly state the function?
3. Is there a clear determination of relationships to any parent organization?
4. Is it distinct from the mission statements of other groups in the organization?
5. Is it short, to the point, and understandable?
6. Is it continuing in nature?
7. Does it state to whom the organization is accountable?

While the word "service" is often included in the mission statement of many organizations, fundamentally the purpose statement needs to answer specifically the question of why your organization is needed in the first place. Plenty of other organizations exist. For example, in light of the "Hospital Code of Ethics" adopted by the American Hospital Association in 1956, a relevant statement of purpose for a hospital system could include wording along the following lines:

> Recognizing that the care of the sick is their first responsibility and a sacred trust, our hospital must at all times strive to provide the best possible care and treatment to all in need of hospitalization. Cognizant of our unique role of safeguarding our region's health, we will seek through compassionate, scientific care and health education to extend life, alleviate suffering, and improve the general health of the community we serve.

In answering the "for whom" question, a purpose statement can reflect whether the HCO wants to be local, regional, national, or international. For example, the mission statement of the Arthritis Foundation chapter noted earlier seeks to support the national organization's goals on a regional basis.

VISION STATEMENTS

We have argued that a comprehensive mission statement captures not only the present identity of the organization but also what the firm hopes to be in the future. Recently, however, this latter, forward-looking aspect of an organization's purpose has received special emphasis with the concept of a vision statement.

A vision statement seeks to focus on the aspirations of the organization. It identifies and clarifies what the organization hopes to become as it fulfills its mission. While the vision statement should be anchored by the firm's heritage and current capabilities, it should move beyond current reality. An organization's vision describes basic future characteristics of the firm. It focuses on the "stretch" the HCO is looking for in its operations to be more than it currently is.

In this context, a vision statement represents a bridge between the mission statement, which expresses the ongoing fundamental reason for which the organization exists, and strategic objectives (discussed in Chapter 5), which provide specific benchmarks for measuring progress toward mission fulfillment. The vision statement identifies broad long-term goals that the HCO hopes to achieve that link its mission with its measurable objectives.

More so than any numerical objective, the vision statement's descriptions should be memorable and inspirational. The vision should be collectively challenging and motivational, moving your staff to take initiative in those gray areas where no policy exists because to do so is to express in a tangible way what you want to be as an organization.

An effective vision statement clearly and concisely describes what the organization hopes to become and how the organization will be viewed by its public(s). Fundamental to a vision statement are descriptions regarding excellence in certain operational areas. For example, an excellence statement as part of a vision for a home healthcare agency might be "constantly seeking the very finest quality home health service delivery."

Also central to an HCO's vision is its anticipation of its reputation for service with its stakeholders. A medical clinic might incorporate as part of its vision a statement such as "to be known as the provider of choice in sports medicine in our region."

In comparing mission, vision, and objectives, mission statements are the longest-term and the least specifically measurable. Objectives are the shortest-term of the three and the most measurable. Vision statements are somewhere in between. They rarely have any numbers included in them. For instance, an objective might state that the organization wants to increase the number of services delivered by 10 percent within the next 12 months. A vision statement, in contrast, might say that "taking care of our patients is everyone's business. Act on this first." Beyond the objectives and even the mission itself, vision statements stand as touchstones to rely upon in an otherwise turbulent environment for certain central aspects of the organization's operation.

SUMMARY

Hopefully, you have caught the significance of verbalizing and putting in writing the vision the leadership of your HCO has for its operation. By committing it to writing, you have, in effect, expressly stated the unique reason for your organization's existence. This provides the sense of identity, direction, and focus for what you do. What you do must be a function of who you are. Statements of purpose and vision translate your firm's long-run dreams and aspirations into tangible form and build a stronger foundation for their fulfillment.

REFERENCES

1. Drucker, Peter. *Management: Tasks, Responsibilities, and Practice* (New York: Harper & Row), 1974, p. 79.

2. Ibid., p. 75.

3. Excerpt from corporate documents of the SunHealth Alliance, Charlotte, North Carolina. Used with permission.

4. Young, Heather M., and Sue T. Hegyvary. "Progress Report on a 'Continuum of Care' Partnership," *Nursing Homes* (November/December, 1993), pp. 29-30.

5. Foley, Brian J. "Nursing Homes' New Goal for the 90's," *Nursing Homes,* (January/February, 1994), pp. 6,8.

6. Excerpt adapted from information supplied by Supportive HomeCare, Ltd., Strategic Plan, 1995, Oshkosh, Wisconsin. Used with permission.

7. 1995 mission and vision statements from documents of the New Orleans Regional Office of the Department of Veterans Affairs. Used with permission.

8. Statement provided by the organization. The organization prefers to remain unidentified. Its mission statement has been modified only where necessary to respect this request. Used with permission.

MISSION AND VISION STATEMENTS WORKSHEET

This worksheet will aid you in writing mission and vision statements for your healthcare organization.

Mission statement

1. Write a statement for the following areas:

   Internal operations statement: ______________________________

   ____

   ____

   ____

   External clientele statement: ______________________________

   ____

   ____

   ____

   Needs served statement: ______________________________

   ____

   ____

   ____

2. Now evaluate the statement.

   Does it define boundaries within which your healthcare organization will operate?

   ____

   ____

   ____

   Does it define the need(s) that your HCO is attempting to meet?

   ____

   ____

   ____

Does it reflect what kind of organization you need to be in order to achieve success in the future?

____

____

____

Do you intend to have local, regional, national, or international scope?

____

____

____

Does it define the market (patients/customers/clientele) that your HCO is reaching?

____

____

____

Has there been input from appropriate organizational members?

____

____

____

Does it include the word "service," or a word with similar meaning?

____

____

____

3. Next, submit it to others familiar with your organization to evaluate your statement of purpose and offer suggestions on improving the statement. In other words, does the statement say to others what you want it to say?

____

____

____

Vision statement

1. Write statements which answer the following questions:

   What do we want our organization to be like in the future?

   ___

   ___

   ___

   What do we want to be known for in the future?

   ___

   ___

   ___

   In what areas of our operation do we aspire to be the very best?

   ___

   ___

   ___

   What do we want our employees to do in achieving the above?

   ___

   ___

   ___

2. Evaluate the vision statement.

   Are the statements clearly phrased and understandable to all the HCO's employees?

   ___

   ___

   ___

Are the statements actively phrased in order to generate energy and enthusiasm within the organization?

____

____

____

Are the statements concise and memorable?

____

____

____

Chapter 4

Situation Analysis and Assumptions

You can never plan the future by the past.

Edmund Burke

If you think what exists today is permanent and forever true, you inevitably get your head handed to you.

John Reed
Chairman, Citicorp

This chapter discusses the need to analyze the situation confronting your healthcare organization and to identify any assumptions on which the strategic plan will be based. We will first discuss the need to assess the environment within which the HCO operates to understand the nature of external influences. Next, the role of internal analysis of the situation within the healthcare organization will be addressed. It is critical that all attributes (whether strengths or weaknesses) of the organization be understood as well as features of its external environment (consisting of opportunities and threats) in order to establish appropriate assumptions on which to develop plans. Consequently, this step in strategic planning is critical to the success of the process.

EXTERNAL ANALYSIS

It is vital for your HCO to gauge the external environment within which it operates. This should be standard practice for all organizations. It is important to realize that virtually anything that *can* happen eventually probably *will* happen. Humans truly can have no certain idea what things will be like in the future, in spite of our attempts to predict them. But your organization cannot afford to let generalized eventualities and uncertainties keep you from being proactive in strategic planning and changing in response to environmental demands.

The only way we can manage change is to constantly monitor the environment within which we operate. Examples for a healthcare organization might be the trends we see in Medicare or Medicaid funding, governmental regulations on funding retirement programs, the labor supply for healthcare professionals, interest rates for capital improvements, more-educated clients/patients expecting to be included in decisions on their healthcare, greater emphasis on marketing healthcare services, the fast pace of technological change, and so forth.

This stage in the analysis is where we look at past and current developments external to our HCO's operations. From this we identify trends and, in effect, take the pulse of the environment in which the HCO operates. External analysis should not be confused with an assumption base, which will be discussed later.

An HCO must be aware of characteristics of environmental conditions affecting it and be vigilant concerning changes that may occur in this environment. There are numerous possible shifts that can occur to affect the firm in categories such as: patients/clients; the general economy; governmental regulation at federal, state, and local levels; sociocultural trends in demographics and lifestyles; and so forth. Many HCOs have found that they failed to understand the implications of the environment on their actions and may not have heeded them, even when they were obvious. Even without a formal organizational system to monitor the environment and changes in it, executives must exercise vigilance to detect and use information from the environment in formulating strategy.

Significance of Environmental Considerations

Organizational Failure May Result

Most management experts agree that any HCO, even one that is extremely successful, will be doomed to ultimate failure if it operates the way it has in the past. Why? Because the environment in which the organization operates is continually shifting and those factors leading to success in one environmental milieu may cause failure in another set of environmental circumstances.

Changes Will Occur

Many of the environmental factors influencing the organization and its administration will change. This is a given. Few factors stand still for long. Thus, the HCO administrator must expect change and should be receptive to it.

For instance, physician practices, once fairly stable operations, face a much more turbulent environment. The advent of more and more expensive technology, a glut of physicians in certain specialties, the movement toward larger group practices, and even the trends toward physician advertising present a much more complicated environment for medical practice.[1] Environmental volatility for physician practices is perhaps most evident, however, in the dramatic moves away from traditional, stand-alone physician groups to managed care networks. Here vertically aligned alliances position physician practices as a component in a larger continuum of care managed by a central organization.

Failure to be responsive to such changes means potentially less effective delivery of healthcare services. Other HCOs face similar brave new worlds, with the consequences of inaction equally as dire.

Environmental Change Will Accelerate

The environment used to be considered an arena in which change was *evolutionary.* Today, however, changes are coming increasingly swiftly. We are now in a situation where changes could be considered *revolutionary.* One has only to look at the technological environment to appreciate this rapid pace of change.

Recent significant management books, as evidenced by their titles, are indicative of this rapid change. Peter Drucker called this the Age of Discontinuity,[2] and Alvin Toffler coined the term for the psychological condition a chaotically changing environment brings about in *Future Shock.*[3] Only now it is present shock.

Changes Will Be Significant

Environmental changes are certain to be significant. In every facet of the environment, significant changes are afoot. Federal budget woes, rising healthcare costs, increasing numbers of aged Americans, litigious tendencies throughout the population, employment cutbacks/layoffs, and worldwide recession all signify significant changes that are occurring in the United States and the rest of the world.

Environmental Factors for Analysis

The environmental circumstances under which the organization is operating and will be operating in the future must be explicitly and carefully considered in any effective strategic planning. Given the nature of the environment, the HCO executive makes judgments about *opportunities* and *threats* facing the organization. The opportunities must be capitalized upon and the threats avoided, minimized, or overcome in order to reach the organization's goals.

The external environmental analysis should evaluate at least seven factors:

1. Economic trends in your locality, in your geographic region, and in the nation. Examples of these trends are changes in personal income, employment, inflation, land values, and industry location.
2. Demographic trends, including shifts in age groups, education levels, numbers of widowed and retired people, and shifts of population to different geographic areas.
3. Community issues of shifts in patient/client bases: urban versus suburban development, growth or decline of commercial activities, and changes in the quantity and quality of transportation services available to potential clientele.
4. Changes in the services offered to people in the community. Who is offering them? Are services shifting primarily into governmental hands or private sponsorship? Are the new sponsors locally owned or national chains? How effective are these services in meeting the needs of the community?

5. Trends in competition from other HCOs for patients, for funding, and for services that may overlap. What other things are going on that present you with competition at this time?
6. Trends in the supply of healthcare professionals in the community and region and reasons for changes in these trends. What HCO activities are the most needed and the best reimbursed, and how will they be staffed now and in the future?
7. Changes in patient/client needs and social values. Are your services what your clients truly need or will want? Apart from basic needs, how well do your services meet clients' expectations? What do people in your community consider important? Are the services you offer and how they are delivered valued?

As an example, a portion of an environmental analysis for a nursing home/extended care facility might include the following trends:

- The graying of America means more people under Medicare coverage as the baby boomers begin to reach old age. Demand for gerontology-related services will increase in parallel with this trend. People are living longer, driving the demand for extended care services upward.
- Federal government reimbursement for Medicare patients is trending down and is likely to continue so as efforts continue on balancing the federal budget. This complicates revenue planning and negatively impacts financial viability.
- Discussion of federal national health insurance programs is rampant in Washington, DC. Congressional enactment could cause radical changes in reimbursement, if not delivery, of healthcare services.
- The costs of medical care have outpaced inflation for two decades and continue to do so. Questions of access to extended care center around this trend. Insurance companies are increasingly emphasizing their product offerings in this area. Pressures will increase to control operating costs and will require new information systems capable of tracking costs by physician, as well as by diagnosis.
- Pressures for cost containment by major payers for healthcare will further encourage trends toward managed care where

nursing homes/extended care facilities will be part of larger care networks. Loose alliances and formal joint ventures with other major providers, such as hospitals and physician groups, will become more commonplace.

- Pressures for lower operating costs will encourage the search for labor cost reductions. Yet paying for credentialed staff is expensive. Increasingly, less credentialed and less expensive staff will be called upon to perform more sophisticated services at some risk to service quality and potential litigation.
- Companies are using more part-time workers and cutting benefits costs by not offering health insurance. Fewer still offer coverage options for long-term care.
- The rising costs of hospital inpatient care encourage earlier patient discharge to lesser cost facilities. This raises demand for extended care beds but means the transferred patients are indeed sicker and require more care.
- Stand-alone facilities are facing increasing competition from extended care chains for the paying patient. They can buy in volume to control costs, whereas stand-alone institutions cannot generate equivalent discounts with their lower usage.

Assessing Opportunities and Threats

Opportunities and threats related to the external environment are analyzed to determine if any action (strategy) is needed to deal with them. For example, a nursing center may notice the move toward hospice programs for the terminally ill. While the hospice philosophy encourages a stay-at-home approach for the dying, there are often needs for short-term interim institutional care to manage complicated medication regimens. The nursing center could offer such institutional services at lower costs than the traditional inpatient, acute care hospital. The patients benefit from the lower charges and the nursing center from increased utilization. Alternatively, the nursing center may decide it does not have the staffing expertise or pharmaceutical services to extend the service, even though the opportunity exists. In either case, opportunities cannot be pursued if they are not recognized and analyzed.

The same is true for threats. An HCO already in trouble from inadequate funding and in heavy debt would face even greater risks if it lost a key leader to illness or death without any preparation for a replacement. The "halo" effect of bad publicity regarding the management and expenses of other HCOs may also be a threat to the existence or at least the effectiveness of the healthcare organization. Recognizing such threats and analyzing the possible ramifications of events helps avoid many crises by developing contingency plans for dealing with such situations. Some have referred to this as "what if" and "what then" analysis. In other words, asking the questions "What if this happens?" and then "What do we do if this happens?" helps an HCO deal with major events that might be detrimental to the organization.

The more you know about the people being served, the better you can meet their needs. Thus the HCO's patient/client base should be a prime element for study. Here, it is useful to build a database. Many successful businesses, such as Wal-Mart, are continually doing research to learn more about their customers. An HCO should do the same thing. Information can be gathered on such factors as marital status, family size, ages of family members, occupations, housing, means of transportation, healthcare needs, reasons for using the HCO's services, and length of time using the HCO's services. All of these are good subjects to ask questions and gather information about.

Scanning the environment of your HCO's operation for significant trends, especially in changing times, is an ongoing effort. This stage in the planning process cannot be just gathering data, getting it on paper, and forgetting about it. The environment must be constantly monitored to help ensure your HCO's survival and growth.

INTERNAL ANALYSIS

After you have identified your HCO's purpose and considered the environment in which you operate, it is important to objectively assess the strengths and weaknesses of your organization's internal operations. HCO administrators need to learn from athletic coaches in this area. Coaches constantly assess the strengths and weaknesses of their team and the opponent. They try to maximize their strengths on game day, and during practice remedy their weaknesses.

Organizations have certain strengths that make them uniquely suited to carry out their tasks. Conversely, they have certain weaknesses that inhibit their abilities to fulfill their purposes. HCOs that seek greater effectiveness need to carefully evaluate the strengths and weaknesses of their organizations.

Identifying strengths and weaknesses within the organization involves a thorough internal analysis, or strategic audit, of the organization. A complete study of the HCO's emphasis on its services and how well they are delivered is the goal. In looking for strengths and weaknesses in the functioning of your organization, a strength is some significant aspect of your operations that is done exceedingly well. What we mean by significant operational aspect is some fundamental activity that is highly likely to affect the performance of your HCO in a major way. Conversely, a weakness is some inadequacy in a major activity or resource that reduces the organization's ability to achieve its goals.

Several different benchmarks can be used to identify whether an activity should be considered a strength or a weakness. One internal standard is how well this activity meets its operational goals when compared to other major functions. This comparison can be made over time to establish trends in effectiveness. Another standard is how well your HCO handles this activity when compared with this function in other HCOs that might be considered your immediate competitors. This is called a strategic group comparison. Another important benchmark for HCOs in particular is how well the activity contributes to the HCO's ability to satisfy the expectations of funding sponsors. But perhaps the most fundamental standard is how well this activity meets the immediate and long-term needs and interests of your patients.

Assessing Strengths and Weaknesses: The Search for a Distinctive Competence

The definitive goal of an internal strengths-and-weaknesses analysis is to identify a distinctive competence. A distinctive competence is some function that you do extraordinarily well. It represents a level of mastery that makes your HCO extremely effective in meeting client needs, particularly when we consider the typical effectiveness of our strategic group in this area of operation. In other words, a distinctive competence is a superstrength that gives us an edge in serving patients' needs and delivering patient satisfaction.

A systematic way to identify strengths and weaknesses is to divide your HCO's operations into major sectors for analysis. Depending on the specific nature of your organization, some basic categories for internal analysis include overall management effectiveness and company resources, financial operations, marketing operations, and production operations or service functions. A good place to begin is with the management of the HCO and its planning systems.

Management and Planning Systems

A specific target of a strengths-and-weaknesses analysis should be a study of the management system. Management's willingness to take risks and their values, skills, ages, and experience are all important aspects of an organization's ability to respond to opportunities. Identifying the effectiveness of an HCO's human resources management is also an objective of this portion of the analysis. This can include issues of how well the firm is organized as well as staff turnover and the recruitment and morale of healthcare professionals.

For instance, the demographics of our professional staff are important in understanding the potential effectiveness of our service capabilities. Appropriate questions include the following: What are the basic staffing categories by profession requiring our attention? How many professionals do we have in each category by age group? What percentage of professional staff will be retiring in the near future? What is the nature of demand and supply for these professionals that will affect the level of recruiting competition?

Still another target for analysis concerns our organization's culture or personality. The following questions deal with the organizational culture profile of our HCO: Are we conservative or liberal in our service philosophy? Are we patient/client-driven or do we focus more on our third-party payers' or financial sponsors' expectations? Does our HCO collaborate with other community agencies and institutions? As an HCO, what are our primary interests and social values? What is the power structure of our HCO? Who really make the decisions and by what process?

Also important to analyze is the effectiveness of our present programs. What are they? Is the leadership for each program effective? How much interest and support does each program have? A management questionnaire can be developed that provides information on the effectiveness of the management system and brings major problems to the surface.

Another target of this analysis is the planning system. Is planning undertaken systematically and performed on a regular basis? Are contingency plans considered? Are the plans realistic? Are they in fact used? All are important issues. Again, a questionnaire can be used to identify and review the planning environment and process, organizational structure, management philosophy and style as it relates to planning, and other factors relating to the organization's performance.

The result is a thorough understanding of the planning system. The data collected in the audit can then be analyzed to determine strengths and weaknesses in the planning system. The most important are then included in a strengths-and-weaknesses summary as a portion of the overall strategic audit. In a similar fashion, the following sectors can be analyzed, using surveys, and the major findings incorporated into the audit.

Financial Resources

The total amount of financial resources an organization has available and the process through which these funds are allocated influence the organization's ability to function effectively. For some organizations there are virtually insurmountable financial barriers. Not only are capital needs extensive, but other expenditures are at a high level. Adequate financial resources must be available to ensure the provision of adequate production and marketing capabilities or the organization must have easy access to funding sources before some ventures can be undertaken.

In many cases, adequate initial financial resources are needed to operate for the first few years while enough paying patients/clients or funding sponsors are developed to sustain an operation. Low revenue levels and high operating costs during the first few years must be anticipated. It goes without saying that unless the financial resources to permit continued operation are available, failure can be anticipated. Thus, an organization's current financial position, plus its ability to successfully obtain financing, directly influence its ability to pursue opportunities.

Specifically, financial resources of the HCO, including operating funds, special funds, donations, and expenditures, should be analyzed. Appropriate questions include "What has been our performance over the last five years in adhering to budget limits?" and "What is our ability to raise funds when needed?" Other specific targets for analysis include break-even points, cash flow, and debt-to-asset ratios.

Marketing Resources

An organization's ability to take advantage of opportunities requires personnel with the marketing skills necessary to develop and execute effective marketing strategies. A good service does not guarantee success. The old adage "Build a better mousetrap and the world will beat a path to your door" is just not true. An HCO must get its message across if it is to thrive.

This requires good marketing, and good marketing is the result of good marketers. Many organizations that were successful in previous time periods have failed in the new environment because of a lack of marketing know-how. If a firm does not have adequate marketing skills available within its own organization, its financial resources must be sufficient to acquire the marketing personnel needed.

Operations/Services Resources

Several distinctly different production resource elements affect a firm's ability to handle new opportunities–service capacity, cost structure, technology, and personnel skills. Capacity is influenced by previous commitments to acquire facilities. In the short run this capacity is usually fixed, but it can be altered, over time, for new strategic opportunities. The skills of personnel available during the short run are also considered fixed. Therefore a firm must have both the capacity and the skills on hand or it must have the financial ability to acquire them. The cost structure of a firm can be a determining factor for some opportunities. The ability or lack of ability to deliver services in a cost-efficient manner can determine an HCO's staying power. Technological capabilities must also be considered. Some new services may require technology not currently available in the organization. If the technology cannot be acquired at a reasonable cost, some opportunities may have to be foregone.

Some appropriate equipment and space questions include the following: Are equipment and space adequate for present needs and for planned future needs? Are they in good operating condition? Are they costly to maintain or operate?

It is relatively easy to identify the strengths in each of these areas. When you attempt to define weaknesses, it becomes a little more painful. Often, organizations must call in outside consultants to be able to candidly pinpoint their limitations. Despite the restraints of organizational politics, weaknesses and limitations must be recognized before you move on. The process should result in all the evaluations listed in the internal analysis being separated into strengths and weaknesses.

HCO planning groups often first identify strengths and write them on a blackboard. After discussions that may list many strengths by organizational function (e.g., marketing, operations, and so on), members of the group agree on perhaps five major strengths. They then have each person write on paper two or three of the organization's weaknesses, which are copied onto the board to generate discussion. Only with an objective appraisal of strengths and weaknesses can realistic objectives be set.

USING A SWOT ANALYSIS

The process of reviewing an HCO's internal operations for strengths and weaknesses and scanning the organization's external environment for opportunities and threats is called a SWOT analysis. As was noted in Chapter 2, SWOT is an acronym for *s*trengths, *w*eaknesses, *o*pportunities, and *t*hreats.

Ultimate goals of a SWOT analysis include, on the one hand, the matching of vital operational strengths with major environmental opportunities. On the other hand, a SWOT analysis provides a basis for eliminating our weaknesses or at least minimizing them and avoiding or managing environmental threats to our operations. Ideally, a SWOT study helps identify a distinctive competence that can be used to tap an important opportunity in our HCO's environment, allowing us to effectively fulfill our strategic objectives and our ongoing mission as an organization.

Exhibit 4.1 illustrates one format for evaluating internal strengths and weaknesses in light of external opportunities by taking into consideration the application of major organizational resources. Each factor–capacity, personnel, marketing, finance, and management–is rated in relation to an opportunity on a quantitative basis.

Exhibit 4.1 Healthcare Organization Resource Evaluation Matrix

	Rating				
	Very Good (1)	Good (2)	Fair (3)	Poor (4)	Very Poor (5)
Operations/Services					
Production Capacity	______	______	______	______	______
Cost Structure	______	______	______	______	______
Technology	______	______	______	______	______
Personnel Skills	______	______	______	______	______
Production	______	______	______	______	______
Operations Score	______	______	______	______	______
Marketing					
Marketing Skills	______	______	______	______	______
Facilities	______	______	______	______	______
Location	______	______	______	______	______
Marketing Score	______	______	______	______	______
Finance					
Fixed Capital Requirements	______	______	______	______	______
Working Capital Requirements	______	______	______	______	______
Finance Score	______	______	______	______	______
Managerial					
Number	______	______	______	______	______
Depth	______	______	______	______	______
Experience	______	______	______	______	______
Managerial Score	______	______	______	______	______
Total Score	______	______	______	______	______

Source: Adapted from Stewart H. Rowoldt, James R. Scott, and Martin R. Warshaw. *Introduction to Marketing Management* (Homewood, Il: Richard D. Irwin, Inc., 1977), pp. 257, 261.

An alternate approach is to analyze these resources as strengths or weaknesses in relation to opportunities in the HCO's environment. This approach is shown in Exhibit 4.2. For each strength and weakness identified, strategy implications are drawn.

Analysis of strengths and weaknesses flows logically from the identification of the resources relative to the opportunity. Each resource, when evaluated within this framework, can be labeled as a strength or weakness, and the implications of that strength or weakness for a specific opportunity can be evaluated.

Exhibit 4.2. Analysis of Strengths and Weaknesses

Factor	Opportunity Implication
A. Marketing resources	
1. Strengths:	
Established facilities	New service could use the same facilities
2. Weaknesses:	
No in-house advertising	Service needs strong advertising effort; use outside ad agency
B. Financial resources	
1. Strengths:	
Good cash position and strong earnings	Consider new service offerings
2. Weaknesses:	
Higher than average debt/asset ratio	Must fund through internal sources
C. Service capacity	
1. Strengths	
High quality operations	Offer additional sophisticated services
2. Weaknesses:	
Low professional staff	Restricts new service offerings
D. Managerial resources	
1. Strengths:	
Strong planning	Cost -effectiveness in operations
2. Weaknesses:	
No experience with new service	Consider alternative services

MAKING ASSUMPTIONS

The next step is to make your major assumptions. These should be made about spheres over which you have little or absolutely no control; factors in the external environment. One good place to start is to extend some of the items studied in the external analysis.

Using the environmental trends for a hypothetical home healthcare agency, assumptions for planning and management of the organization might well include such statements as those listed below:

1. Intervention by the federal government in healthcare delivery will continue to escalate. Some major modifications of health insurance coverage will be mandated by Congress within five years.
2. Federal reimbursement for healthcare will continue to drop and philanthropy will largely be a thing of the past.
3. Employers will take an increasingly aggressive stance as healthcare purchasers in trying to control the costs of healthcare benefits for their employees.
4. Technological advances will continue at an ever-increasing pace. Many will continue to be expensive, but others will represent competition to traditional in-house services as more over-the-counter tests are approved for direct public use.
5. The relatively high cost of traditional inpatient hospital care will cause physicians to admit more patients directly to home care programs without prior hospital stays.
6. Capitated (limited enrollment) reimbursement programs will escalate, changing hospitals from profit centers to cost centers and encouraging greater linkages with less expensive home healthcare services.
7. Managed care companies will proliferate with the general mandate to cut delivery costs significantly, often by moving patients with cardiology, respiratory, diabetic, and pregnancy conditions into home care settings sooner.[4]

A similar list should be developed of certain assumptions that characterize strategic aspects of your particular HCO's operation. Assumptions are those situational trends that in our estimate will significantly impact our HCO's activities during the period being planned for. Major considerations include the nature of our patients'/clients' expectations, our funding sources, and our competitors. Although these assumptions are largely outside our sphere of influence, they are basic beginning points for the HCO's plans for future delivery of services.

Here are some general assumptions that fit the strategic planning model:

1. Quality leads to quantity. The quality of service leads to expansion of services. Higher quality of services leads to greater demand for services.
2. A commitment to excellence produces confidence in the HCO's leadership and administration. If the administration is committed to excellence and demonstrates it in its leadership style, then the professional staff and other constituents will feed off this confidence, allowing them to persevere in uncertain situations.
3. Sponsorship and funding of the HCO will continue to be a challenge, but continued effort will produce sources of funds, sometimes from new and unexpected directions.
4. Each service offered has some unique aspects to it that may require new ways of doing things. Policies and procedures should be adapted to produce the best results, not just standardization.
5. Improving the efficiency of your HCO's operations should not be such an overwhelming focus that staff lose sight of the inherent good to society the HCO seeks to provide.

Assumptions must be directly related to action. Note the relationship between assumption and proposed action in the following example for nursing homes:

Assumption– The costs of extended care will receive even more scrutiny as the demand for services escalates.

As managed care companies increasingly blanket the healthcare marketplace, they will seek to find cost-saving measures wherever possible. Many will look for nursing homes with lower cost structures to provide more sophisticated services to their subacute patients.

Action– Bring in a TQM consultant with healthcare industry experience to begin a TQM program.

Increasingly, total quality management (TQM) techniques will be used to deliver quality extended care at lower costs. Applying TQM techniques in service industries is a challenging task. Yet an environmental analysis of the healthcare industry reveals that more and more HCOs are taking up the gauntlet.

Nursing homes are part of this trend, but the techniques are often foreign to these providers. Despite this newness, an industry analysis shows that nursing home TQM programs need to be developed to keep up with the competition that is also developing TQM programs. Reimbursement pressures also bear on the need to pursue the cost savings associated with TQM.

TQM requires the full endorsement of senior management and their training in program techniques. Beyond this, cross-functional teams need to be developed to focus on patient care plans and diagnosis categories that offer the potential for earlier discharge. TQM's customer satisfaction orientation may steer extended care facilities away from a top-of-the-line-amenities strategy toward a greater focus on improving the patient's health to the point of returning the patient home–a seemingly universal desire for all patients.[5] This level of change in delivery of care typically calls for an expert in interventions such as TQM.

The key is knowing what is going on and being alert to opportunities. Next, develop a full plan based on a few assumptions. If an assumption changes, the plan changes.

The worksheet at the end of this chapter (which appears again in Appendix A) is a useful tool for internal and external analysis. Answering all the questions can be a good start in assessing your organization in several areas. To further help you in making these external assessments, Appendix C contains several sample client surveys that can be modified for use by your organization.

SUMMARY

This chapter has emphasized the importance of coming to grips with the external and internal environments in which you must work to fulfill your mission. Minimizing weaknesses and capitalizing on strengths helps bolster the ability of an organization to operate in its external environment. Specifying the assumptions provides a basis for thoughtful consideration of the basic premises on which you operate. They should also cause you to ponder the "what if/what then" scenarios that, through contingency planning, help avoid disruptions in the organization's operations.

REFERENCES

1. Henthorne, Beth Hogan, and Tony L. Henthorne. "Identifying and Removing the Barriers to Strategic Marketing Planning Within Medical Practices," *Health Marketing Quarterly,* Vol. 11(1/2), 1993, pp. 59-74.

2. Drucker, Peter F. *The Age of Discontinuity: Guidelines to Our Changing Society* (New York: Harper & Row), 1969.

3. Toffler, Alvin. *Future Shock* (New York: Random House), 1970.

4. Lumsdon, Kevin. "No Place Like Home?" *Hospitals and Health Networks* (October 4, 1994), pp. 44-52.

5. Lumsdon, Kevin. "Ready for More Managed Care?" article within "No Place Like Home?" *Hospitals and Health Networks* (October 4, 1994), p. 48.

SITUATION ANALYSIS AND ASSUMPTIONS WORKSHEET

This worksheet will aid you in completing a Strengths, Weaknesses, Opportunities, and Threats (SWOT) analysis.

Step 1. **External Environment Analysis:** From industry surveys and your own sources of information, take your organization's pulse. You are looking for trends–what is going on now and how this relates to past trends that have influenced your HCO's performance. From this analysis, list key opportunities and threats for each of the following environmental sectors.

Government

Opportunities

1. ______________________________
2. ______________________________
3. ______________________________

Threats

1. ______________________________
2. ______________________________
3. ______________________________

Economy

Opportunities

1. ______________________________
2. ______________________________
3. ______________________________

Threats

1. ______________________________
2. ______________________________
3. ______________________________

Technology

Opportunities

1. ______________________________
2. ______________________________
3. ______________________________

Threats

1. ______________________________
2. ______________________________
3. ______________________________

Social Trends

Opportunities

1. ______________________________
2. ______________________________
3. ______________________________

Threats

1. ______________________________
2. ______________________________
3. ______________________________

Patients/Clients

Opportunities

1. ______________________________
2. ______________________________
3. ______________________________

Threats

1. ______________________________
2. ______________________________
3. ______________________________

Reimbursement Sources/Sponsorship

Opportunities

1. ______________________________
2. ______________________________
3. ______________________________

Threats

1. ______________________________
2. ______________________________
3. ______________________________

Competing HCOs

Opportunities

1. ______________________________
2. ______________________________
3. ______________________________

Threats

1. ______________________________
2. ______________________________
3. ______________________________

Next, evaluate your external analysis:

Have you listed several international/national trends that affect your HCO?

____

____

____

Have you listed several local trends that affect your HCO?

____

____

____

Have you identified trends unique to your HCO (e.g., availability of certain healthcare professionals)?

____

____

____

Have you listed several of your most important competitors?

____

____

____

Which are growing? ______________________________

____

Which are declining? ______________________________

____

What are the successful ones doing? ______________________________

____

Step 2. **Internal Operations Analysis:** Using the question guides below and your own information, list key strengths and weaknesses for each of the following sectors of your HCO's operations.

Management and Planning Systems

Use these questions to help you prepare your strengths and weaknesses list for this portion of your HCO's operation.

Do you have a planning system?

____

____

____

How does it work?

____

____

____

Is the organizational structure of your HCO allowing effective use of resources?

Is control centralized or decentralized?

Are performance measures and information system controls in evidence? What are they?

What staffing needs do you have?

Is there a motivation problem?

Is your current strategy defined? Is it working?

How efficient are operations?

What is your synopsis of the current management situation?

___

___

___

Now list your strengths and weaknesses for this section of your HCO's operations.

Strengths

___

___

___

Weaknesses

___

___

___

Financial Resources

Use these questions to help you prepare your strengths and weaknesses list for this portion of your HCO's operation.

What is your current financial situation?

___

___

___

Do you have regular financial statements prepared?

___

___

___

What tools would be beneficial in analysis?

___

___

___

Do you have pro forma statements for revenue centers such as rehabilitative care, hospice care, etc.?

Do you have a cash budget?

Do you have a capital budget?

Has a ratio analysis been prepared?

Do you understand the time value of money?

Do you understand and use break-even analysis?

Have you analyzed current financial policies?

Do you have cash policies?

How are accounts receivable analyzed?

How are accounts payable analyzed?

Do you control inventory levels?

Do you have a debt retirement plan?

Give a synopsis of your current financial situation.

Accounting analysis:

Depreciation procedures?

Tax considerations?

Decentralized/centralized operations? ______________________________

____

Responsibility accounting?___________________________________

____

Tools beneficial in analysis:

Do you have budgets (short- and long-range) established?

____

____

____

Do you perform variance analysis comparing actual against planned performance?

____

____

____

What costing methods are used?

____

____

____

Do you do contribution margin analysis?

____

____

____

Are there adequate controls, especially of cash, for each of your HCO's programs?

____

____

____

What is your synopsis of the current accounting situation?

Now list your strengths and weaknesses for this section of your HCO's operations.

Strengths

Weaknesses

Marketing Resources

Use these questions to help you prepare your strengths and weaknesses list for this portion of your HCO's operation.

Have you established marketing policies?

Have you established what you will and will not do in marketing your services?

Have you identified your patients/clients?

Have you identified your funding/reimbursement sponsors?

____

____

____

What are your competitors' services and products, level of demand, and relative market positions?

____

____

____

What are your distribution systems and location of facilities and how effective are they?

____

____

____

Is your services' price/fee structure current and appropriate?

____

____

____

What promotion (advertising, sales promotion, and personal selling) activities are you using?

____

____

____

What is your synopsis of the current marketing situation?

____

____

____

Now list your strengths and weaknesses for this section of your HCO's operations.

Strengths

____

____

____

Weaknesses

____

____

____

Operations or Services Resources

What are your operations capacities?

____

____

____

What shape are your facilities in?

____

____

____

What is the age and serviceability of your equipment?

____

____

____

How automated are your operations?

____

____

____

What are your transportation capabilities?

____

____

____

Are safety programs adequate?

____

____

____

How effective is your inventory control?

____

____

____

Do you use quality control systems?

____

____

____

Now list your strengths and weaknesses for this section of your HCO's operations.

<u>Strengths</u>

____

____

____

<u>Weaknesses</u>

____

____

____

Next, evaluate the services of your professional staff:

Range of services offered?

____

____

____

Number of services rendered, patients served by service category?

____

____

____

Number and age of professional staff by service category?

____

____

____

Now, evaluate your internal analysis:

Have you listed and analyzed all major internal factors with significant impact on your organization's operations?

____

____

____

Step 3. **Development of Assumptions:** List the major assumptions on which your plan is based.

1. ____________________________________
2. ____________________________________
3. ____________________________________
4. ____________________________________
5. ____________________________________

Chapter 5

Establishing Organizational Objectives

Ah, but a man's reach should exceed his grasp, or what's a heaven for?

Robert Browning

Not failure but low aim is crime.

J. R. Lowell

In this chapter we will discuss establishing objectives, the third step in the strategic planning process. After the purpose or mission of the healthcare organization has been defined, internal and external analysis completed, and assumptions made, then–and only then–can relevant objectives be considered.

Clearly, one cannot achieve goals if none exist. Although this idea is quite simple, many people overlook it. In order to accomplish anything, we must make up our minds to do it. If we fail to do this first step, we simply waste our time and energy by going in circles. Later, we look back at what we accomplished and wonder where the time went.

NATURE AND ROLE OF OBJECTIVES

Objectives can be defined as clear, concise written statements outlining what is to be accomplished in key areas in a certain time period, in objectively measurable terms. Drucker argues that "objectives are not fate; they are direction. They are not commands, but they are commitments. They do not determine the future, but they are the means by which the resources and energies of the operation can be mobilized for the making of the future."[1]

The words "key results," "goals," and "targets" are often used synonymously when talking about both short- and long-term objectives. Whatever the label used, the idea is to focus on a specific set of target activities and outcomes to be accomplished. Think of the analogy of the archer used earlier. An HCO administrator wants the whole organization aimed at a single target, just as an archer wants every arrow aimed at the bull's-eye. People get confused and disorganized if they do not know where they are going. In large measure, the success or failure of a healthcare organization is based on its ability to set goals, as well as on tools with which to measure progress toward those goals.

Yet there are at least six reasons why HCOs fail to set clear objectives:

1. Many HCO managers fear accountability.
2. Many projects continue even when they no longer serve an organization's goals.
3. HCOs often undertake any activity for which money is available.
4. Some HCO managers fear hard-nosed evaluation may undermine humanitarian instincts.
5. HCO managers must spend a great deal of time on activities that do not immediately further their goals (meeting with donors, fund-raising, explaining programs, and so forth).
6. HCOs may have few, if any, financial report cards to tell them how they are doing.[2]

Once the process of setting objectives is actually begun in the organization, some of the goal-making deterrents mentioned above may no longer be applicable. However, much of this list could be applied in many types of organizational settings.

Objectives can be set at upper organizational levels in key result areas such as range of service offerings, productivity, level of client satisfaction, market share, profitability, financial resources, physical resources, staff development and attitudes, and commitment to social responsibilities as an organization. Every healthcare administrator should consider long-range objectives in each of these areas.

Objectives are also needed in subunits, departments, or divisions of an organization. Objectives can be classified in various ways such as by their nature, including routine, problem solving, and innovative, or by their function, including team, personal, and budget performance. Most important, all organizational objectives must be consistent. Thus, a department's objectives should lead to accomplishing the overall organization's goals.

Objectives serve two fundamental purposes. First, they serve as a road map. Objectives are the results desired upon completion of the planning period. In the absence of objectives, no sense of direction can be attained in decision making. In planning, objectives answer one of the basic questions posed in the planning process: Where do we want to go? These objectives become the focal point for strategy decisions.

Another basic purpose served by objectives is in the evaluation of performance. The objectives in the strategic plan become the yardsticks used to evaluate performance. As will be pointed out later, it is impossible to evaluate performance without some standard by which results can be compared. The objectives become the standards for evaluating performance because they are the statement of results desired by the planner.

Objectives have sometimes been called the neglected area of management. In many situations there is a failure to set objectives, or the objectives that are set forth are unsound and therefore lose much of their effectiveness. To counteract this, a management tool called management by objectives (MBO) was developed. It emphasizes the need for setting objectives as a basic managerial process, providing coordination of activities at all levels of the organization.

For the HCO administrator, management by objective translates into four basic steps.[3] First, the administrator and individual staff work out mutual objectives that each staff member will pursue in his or her area of responsibility. These objectives should support the overall objectives established by the HCO. Each staff member with supervisory responsibilities, in turn, holds similar meetings with his/her staff or volunteers. These meetings should be held at each management level so that objectives are fully coordinated.

Second, in addition to objective-setting at these meetings, strategies or descriptions of actions to be taken to accomplish each objective should be laid out. Third, follow-up meetings should be held periodically to monitor progress toward objectives, identify problems, and mutually determine methods to correct any difficulties. The final step involves an overall evaluation of goal accomplishment for individuals and units at year's end or the end of the planning period. From this, new objectives for the coming planning period can be determined.

ALTERNATIVES TO MANAGEMENT BY OBJECTIVES

One way to be convinced of the usefulness and power of management by objectives is to consider some of the alternatives:[4]

1. *Management by extrapolation (MBE)*–This approach relies on the principle "If it ain't broke, don't fix it." The basic idea is to keep on doing about the same things in about the same ways because what we're doing (1) works well enough and (2) has gotten us where we are. The basic assumption is that, for whatever reason, "Our act is together, so why worry? The future will take care of itself and things will work out all right."
2. *Management by crisis (MBC)*–This approach to administration is based upon the idea that the strength of any really good manager is solving problems. Since there are plenty of crises around–enough to keep everyone occupied–managers ought to focus their time and energy on solving the most pressing problems of today. MBC is, essentially, reactive rather than proactive, and the events that occur dictate management decisions.
3. *Management by subjectives (MBS)*–The MBS approach occurs when no organization-wide consensus or clear-cut directives exist on which way to head and what to do. Each manager translates this to mean "do your best to accomplish what you think should be done." This is a "do your own thing the best way you know how" approach. This is also referred to as "the mystery approach." Managers are left on their own with no clear direction ever articulated by senior management.
4. *Management by hope (MBH)*–In this approach, decisions are predicated on the hope that they will work out and that good times are just around the corner. They are based on the belief

that if you try hard enough and long enough, then things are bound to get better. Poor performance is attributed to unexpected events and the fact that decisions always have uncertainties and surprises. Much time, therefore, is spent hoping and wishing things will get better.

All four of these approaches represent variations of managerial "muddling through." Absent is any effort to calculate what effort is needed to influence where an organization is headed and what its activities should be to reach specific objectives. In contrast, management by objectives is much more likely to achieve targeted results and have a sense of direction.

CHARACTERISTICS OF GOOD OBJECTIVES

For objectives to accomplish their purpose of providing direction and a standard for evaluation, they must possess certain characteristics. The more these attributes are possessed by a given objective, the more likely it will achieve its basic purpose. Sound internal objectives (as opposed to external objectives for public consumption, which may have to be more generalized) should have the following characteristics:

1. Objectives Should Be Clear and Concise

There should not be any room for misunderstanding what results are sought in a given objective. The use of long statements with words or phrases that may be defined or interpreted in different ways by different people should be avoided.

2. Objectives Should Be in Written Form

This helps solve two problems: unclear, ineffective communication and altering unwritten objectives over time. First, everyone who has played the game of "gossip" realizes that oral statements can be unintentionally altered as they are communicated. Written statements avoid this problem and permit ease of communication. A second problem involves the tendency to want to "look good," often at the expense of actual performance. Unwritten objectives can be altered to fit current circumstances.

3. Objectives Should Name Specific Results in Key Areas

The key areas in which objectives are needed were identified earlier. Specific results, such as "5,000 patients treated for the next year" rather than "a high level of patients served" or "an acceptable level of patient services," should be used to avoid doubt about what result is sought.

4. Objectives Should Be Stated for a Specific Time Period

Objectives can be set for a short-run, nearly immediate time period such as six months to one year. Building on longer and longer time frames, accomplishment of short-term objectives should lead to successful completion of longer-run objectives. The time period specified becomes a deadline for producing results and also sets up the final evaluation of the success of a strategy.

5. Objectives Should Be Stated in Measurable Terms

Concepts that defy precise definition and qualification should be avoided. "Patient satisfaction" is an example of a concept that is important, but which in itself is difficult to define and measure. If a planner felt patient satisfaction was a concept that needed to be measured, a measure or measures (possibly indirect in nature) would have to be developed. An objective related to patient satisfaction that would be capable of quantification might be stated as follows: "To have at least 85 percent of our constituents rate our HCO as the best organization in the area in our annual survey." Phrases such as "improve staffing" not only are not clear or specific, but also are statements that cannot be measured. What does "improve" mean? Increase the number of staff by 5 percent? By 40 percent? In what areas? If the statement is quantified as "increase the number of full-time physical therapists by 10 percent within the next 18 months," it can be objectively measured. The accomplishment or failure of such a stated objective can be readily evaluated.

6. Objectives at Each Administrative Level Must Be Consistent with Overall Organizational Objectives and Purpose

This idea has been previously stated, but must be continually reemphasized because of the need for organizational unity.

7. Objectives Should Be Attainable, but of Sufficient Challenge to Stimulate Effort

Two problems can be avoided if this characteristic is achieved. One is the avoidance of frustration produced by objectives that cannot be attained, or that cannot be attained within the specified time period. For instance, large percentage increases in patients served at home can be unrealistic as goals if the home healthcare agency already has an unusually large patient load. The desirability and likelihood of substantial increases become doubtful.

The other problem is setting objectives that are so easy to attain that only minimum effort is needed. This results in performance evaluations that look good from a distance, since every goal is being accomplished, but, in reality, only camouflage lackluster performance well short of potential. Easy goals fail to maximize the contribution of a given strategic plan.

One approach to writing objectives that contain realistic, but challenging, characteristics is to apply a set of criteria to each statement to increase the probability of good objectives. One such list follows:

1. *Relevance.* Are the objectives related to and supportive of the basic purpose of the organization?
2. *Practicality.* Do the objectives take into consideration obvious constraints (such as budgetary limitations)?
3. *Challenge.* Do the objectives provide a challenge?
4. *Measurability.* Are the objectives capable of some form of quantification, if only on an order-of-magnitude basis?
5. *Schedule.* Are the objectives so constituted that they can be time phased and monitored at interim points to ensure progress toward their attainment?
6. *Balance.* Do the objectives provide for a proportional emphasis on all activities and keep the strengths and weaknesses of the organization in proper balance?

Objectives that meet such criteria are much more likely to serve their intended purpose. The resulting statements can then serve as the directing force in the development of strategy. Consider the following examples of poorly stated objectives:

Poor: Our objective is to lower the rate of medication errors.

Remarks: How much is "lower"? The statement is not subject to measurement. What criterion or yardstick will be used to determine if and when actual error rates are equal to those desired? In addition, no deadline is specified.

Better: Our objective is to lower our medication error rate by 10 percent within 12 months.

Poor: Our objective is to increase our occupancy rates.

Remarks: How much? A single patient-per-day increase will meet that objective, but is that really the desired target?

Better: Our objective this calendar year is to increase occupancy rates by 5 percent.

Poor: Our objective is to boost advertising expenditures by 15 percent.

Remarks: Advertising is an activity, not a result. The advertising objective should be stated in terms of what result the extra advertising is intended to produce.

Better: Our objective is to boost patient revenues by 10 percent in each of the next five years with the help of a 15 percent annual increase in advertising expenditures.

Poor: Our objective is to be the best healthcare organization of its type in our area.

Remarks: Not specific enough; what measures of "best" are to be used? Number of patients served? Level of reimbursement? Number of new programs started? Services offered? Number of professional staff?

Better: We will strive to become the number one healthcare organization of its kind in the metropolitan area in terms of the number of patients served within five years.

The following practical suggestions are offered for writing objectives:

1. Objectives should start with an action verb, since the achievement of an objective must come as a result of specific action.
2. Each objective should specify a single major result to be accomplished so the group will know precisely when the objective has been achieved.
3. An objective should have a target date for accomplishment.
4. An objective should relate directly to the mission statement of the group or organization. A local facility of a national nursing home chain should not write an objective outside the scope of its own mission statement or one that pertains more to the mission statement of the parent organization. This may seem obvious, but groups often commit themselves to projects for which they have neither responsibility nor authority.
5. An objective must be understandable to those who will be working to achieve the specified results.
6. An objective must be possible to achieve.
7. An objective should be consistent with parent organization policies and practices.

TYPES OF OBJECTIVES INCLUDED IN A STRATEGIC PLAN

Strategic plans for healthcare organizations usually focus on at least four types of objectives: (1) services offered; (2) staffing; (3) services reimbursement, donations, and funding; and (4) constituents served. However, objectives should be established in *all* key result areas of the HCO's operations. Key result areas are those activities that are most likely to impact the performance of the organization. They are the few things that must go right if the HCO is to be effective and thrive. For example, key result areas for a hospital/clinic could include:

1. Percentage of doctors who are board certified
2. Number and quality of services offered
3. Number of patients served by service: inpatient/outpatient
4. Successful surgery and treatment rates
5. Financial condition/budget status/surplus

6. Status of physical facilities
7. Quality
8. Productivity
9. Patient satisfaction
10. Innovation
11. Percent occupancy rate
12. Number of physicians by specialty
13. Level of professional staffing

Short-term objectives are stated for the operating period only, normally one year, whereas long-term objectives often span five to ten years. For example, five-year objectives can be set in areas such as clients served, programs offered, fund-raising, services offered, and so forth. While the definition of "long term" varies, HCOs should be planning at least as far into the future as present-day obligations commit them. For instance, the planned construction of a new building with a 45-year life means that the organization should be looking 45 to 50 years into the future with regard to the effective use of the facility.

In setting objectives, we first state them in terms of what we want to accomplish, but as we develop the strategy we may discover that we cannot afford what we want. The available resources committed to a given program or service may not be sufficient to achieve a stated objective; and if the planning process is resource-controlled, the objectives must be altered. It must be remembered that objectives are not fate, but they are direction. They are not commands, but they become commitments. As a planner, you must not fall into the trap of thinking that once objectives are set they cannot or should not be altered.

Following are some examples of key result area objectives.

Productivity Objectives

Increasing levels of productivity and cost-effectiveness are essential to the vitality of HCOs such as home healthcare organizations in managed care environments. New staffing patterns, the use of teams to improve care plans, and new information systems are often critical to achieving improved productivity.[5] Objectives for improvements in productivity may be stated numerically or as a percentage of the total number. If the objectives are stated in percentages, they also need to be converted to numbers for budgeting.

Examples of productivity objectives are given in Exhibit 5.1. Each of the objectives in Exhibit 5.1 is clear, concise, and quantifiable, and has a target date. The way objectives are stated must reflect what the organization can realistically expect to attain under a given plan.

Funding Objectives

Funding and reimbursement for services rendered are vital aspects of any HCO's operations, especially in an era when financial sources are drying up. While seeking increased revenues simply for revenues' sake should not be the only end pursued, the need to increase revenues is an inescapable fact of life in order for an HCO to deliver its services. The issue of continued survival offers a very practical reason for developing a specific statement about funding targets. Getting specific about desirable end results forces the planner to estimate the resources needed to underwrite specific programs and services.

A statement of whether resources will be available cannot be made without a break-even analysis on the cost of providing services that must carry their own financial weight. For new programs, the expenditures and contributions associated with the program should be analyzed before introduction. For existing programs, revenues can be analyzed to project continued levels of financial viability. This information, combined with estimates of expenses involved in delivering services, provides a basis for statements of objectives about funding levels.

Sample statements are shown in Exhibit 5.2 as illustrations of financial objectives, in this case for a medical practice. Again, nebulous phrases such as "acceptable revenue levels" or "reasonable debt levels" have been avoided because of the possible variations in definition and the lack of quantifiability.

Exhibit 5.1
Examples of Productivity Objectives by Function

1. Patient Care Services: Reduce the average number of home visits per patient by 10 percent for the coming 12 months over last year's level.
2. Business Office Operations: Reduce paperwork expenses by 15 percent within the next 24 months when compared with the most recent 24-month period.

Exhibit 5.2
Examples of Financial Objectives

1. Increase annual return on gross patient revenues to at least 20 percent by end of year two of planning cycle.
2. Reduce long-term debt to 25 percent of equity within five years.
3. Hold increases in average charges per patient to 8 percent above previous year's average for the coming year.

Keep in mind that the interactive processes of setting objectives and developing strategies must be carried out realistically. The costs of many aspects of strategy cannot be estimated until a written statement of strategy is developed. If the strategy calls for a new program, for example, that strategy must be spelled out in detail before costs can be estimated.

Patient/Client (Customer) Objectives

Patient/client objectives may seem unusual to some, but their inclusion should be obvious. They serve as enabling objectives in areas of productivity and revenue generation. But fundamentally they represent specific statements about the number and level of services the HCO will offer to its customers.

Patient objectives are especially important in providing direction for the development of the strategy section of the plan. As shown in Exhibit 5.3, they specify results desired for constituents by program category. Client objectives should have the same characteristics as other objectives. They must be stated in unambiguously measurable terms and should be evaluated in relation to their accomplishment as a part of the monitoring and control system used in the plan.

USING ENVIRONMENTAL ANALYSIS DATA TO SET OBJECTIVES

The objectives of a given plan are based on the data provided in the situation analysis discussed earlier. In other words, good objectives are based on a careful analysis of the external and internal

Exhibit 5.3
Examples of Patient/Client Service Objectives

1. Develop a wellness program to be fully operational within three years.
2. Complete a plan for the development of an elder care service within six months.

environment of the HCO. A specific example of how data are used in setting objectives may help in understanding this point.

Consider a hypothetical nursing home facility in a city of approximately 400,000 with a desire to expand its services. In a search for opportunities for service expansion, the center has monitored the growth in hospice programs in the community, now numbering five in operation. The nursing home has the physical facilities to expand since one of its older wings is only 20 percent utilized.

The center conducts a survey of the hospice programs to identify potential areas of mutual benefit. Through the survey it learns that at any one time each of the programs has some of its patients hospitalized for interim periods for medication adjustments. The center notes that the only current option for this service is hospitalization. Knowing that its current staff of registered nurses is capable of managing this type of medication service, the nursing home sees an opportunity to improve its utilization while providing a needed service for lower cost than the current hospital inpatient approach. An immediate question arising from this opportunity is how much of a facility commitment would be required for this new service.

The resulting analysis in Exhibit 5.4 demonstrates how this commitment could be estimated.

Objectives derived through such a process represent the realities of the area and also the HCO's willingness and ability to commit itself to such objectives. This example should also reemphasize the logic in the strategic planning format. The analysis precedes setting objectives, because objectives must be based on realistic information that only a careful analysis can provide.

Exhibit 5.4
Potential for Hospice Medication Program

1. Average number of hospice patients across five programs = 150.
2. Average percentage of hospice patients hospitalized for medication management at any one time = 10 percent.
3. Average number of hospice patients at any one time using in-hospital medication management services = 15.
4. Estimated percent of hospice patients receiving medication management whose conditions are uncomplicated enough to allow nursing center delivery of the service = 90 percent.
5. Total average number of hospice medication patients = 13.5 (i.e., 15 x .9).
6. Initial estimated acceptance of the program by referring physicians = 60 percent.
7. Initial viable target market for program = 8.1 patients (i.e., 13.5 x .6).
8. Objective: Initially commit 8 beds to the hospice medication service program.

PERFORMANCE CONTRACTS

Objectives can become the basis of a performance contract for staff members. As an example, note how the objectives for an associate administrator can become a performance contract through the following process:

1. Properly written objectives submitted to the HCO administrator.
2. Items discussed and negotiated with the administrator.
3. Objectives resubmitted to the administrator.
4. List approved by both the associate administrator and the administator (and perhaps the HCO's governing board).
5. In some organizations, both parties sign an objectives sheet, on which the objectives are carefully spelled out in final form.

PERIODIC REVIEW

One practical, easy way to record, communicate, measure, and update objectives is through a "Performance Plan Book" or "Management Plan Book." All objectives for the organization should be in this book. Objectives can be reviewed each quarter and updated. This process greatly reduces paperwork and provides a convenient method for review. Examples of how objectives might be set up in a management plan book are shown in Exhibits 5.5 to 5.7.

Exhibit 5.5
Sample Management Plan Book: Overall Objectives
(use a three-year spread)

	(Year 1)	(Year 2)	(Year3)
PATIENTS SERVED			
Program One			
Program Two			
Program Three			
PHYSICIAN STAFFING			
Program One			
Program Two			
Program Three			
Training Seminars			
FINANCIAL (per existing program)			
Revenues			
New patients			
Budgets			
Current ratio			
Fixed Asset Turnover:			
Revenues/Net Fixed Assets			
Total Asset Turnover:			
Revenues/Total Assets			
Debt Ratio:			
Total Debt/Total Assets			
Dept/Total Revenue			
Times Interest Earned:			
Revenue/Interest			
STAFF			
Administrator			
Assistants			

Exhibit 5.5 (continued)

	(Year 1)	(Year 2)	(Year 3)
BUILDINGS			
Build/Buy/Rent Facilities			
Existing Facilities Improvement			
New Equipment			
Equipment Repair or Replacement			
EXISTING FACILITIES			
Systematic Safety Check			
Heating and Cooling			
Security: Burglar Alarms			
Lighting			
Parking			
Sound System/Other Special Systems			
STAFF TRAINING AND MORALE			
Administrator Education Seminars			
Staff Training: In-House			
Staff Training: External Seminars			
Yearly Attitude Survey			
PUBLIC RESPONSIBILITY			
Cooperative Efforts with Other HCOs			
NEW PROGRAMS (per program)			
Patient Need Assessment			
Competing Programs			
Revenue Sources			
Reimbursement Levels			
Development/Start-Up Expenses			
Operating Budgets			
Staff Required			

Exhibit 5.6
Sample Review Sheet: Management Plan, (year)

Objectives	Results
I. New Program: Set aside $5,000 for consulting for new wellness program.	On Target
II. Budget Performance: Operate within the $2,500,000 budget throughout fiscal (year).	On Target
III. Problem Solving: Develop an efficient transportation routing schedule to be followed for home equipment deliveries by (date).	Met 90%
IV. Innovative: Devise a better layout for patient/staff parking during (month and year).	Done
V. Personal: Read the book, Fundamentals of Strategic Planning for Healthcare Organizations; attend communication course, Fall of (year).	Book completed; course registration mailed

Exhibit 5.7
Sample Objectives for an Administrator:
Administrator's Objectives, (year)

I. Routine Objectives
   1. To make at least one round of patient visits per week.
   2. To review each program's objectives and accomplishments by January 5, May 5, and August 5.
   3. To attend the annual state administrators' meeting

II. Problem-Solving Objectives
   1. To develop a cooperative education linkage with the local college to increase recruiting within the coming year.
   2. To develop staff training seminar by January 31.
   3. To develop a set of criteria and measurable objectives for a professional staff retreat within 6 weeks.
   4. To hold a one-day open house for community education within 3 months.

III. Innovative Objectives
   1. To devise a better system of generating new ideas for prospective service programs within 6 months.
   2. To develop improved information systems for giving all program leaders feedback on their budget performance. Implementation by (date).

IV. Personal Objectives
   1. To improve my understanding of the latest trends in service delivery; visit at least one similar HCO operation every six months.
   2. To exercise four times per week.

V. Team Objectives
   1. To work with the staff on revision and update of public relations brochure to be introduced in July.
   2. To meet with the staff each Wednesday to troubleshoot problems and coordinate activities.

VI. Budget Objectives
   1. To operate within the $1,500,000 yearly budget.
   2. To retire 10 percent of the debt on the building within the next year.

SUMMARY

Setting objectives is another major part of the strategic planning process. The necessity for objectives as well as their characteristics was presented here to lay the groundwork for identifying basic types of objectives for such key result areas as patient services, revenue generation, and operational productivity. The statements of objectives given as examples in this chapter possess the basic characteristics needed to serve both as a source of direction and in evaluation of the strategies developed in the plan.

REFERENCES

1. Drucker, Peter. *The Practice of Management* (New York: Harper, 1954), p. 102.

2. Ibid., p. 102.

3. Muczyk, J. P. and B. C. Reimann. "MBO as a Complement to Effective Leadership," *The Academy of Management Executive,* 3 (1989), pp. 131-138.

4. Adapted from Thompson, Arthur A., Jr., and A. J. Strickland, *Strategy Formulation and Implementation,* 3rd ed. (Plano, Texas: Business Publication, Inc., 1986), p. 52.

5. Lumsdon, Kevin. "Ready for More Managed Care?" Article within "No Place Like Home?" *Hospitals and Health Networks* (October 4, 1994), p. 48.

OBJECTIVES WORKSHEET

This worksheet will aid you in developing objectives for your HCO's operations.

Answer These Questions First

1. What do your objectives need to relate to–patients, services, revenues, professional staffing, other areas? What about other key result areas?

   ____

   ____

   ____

2. What needs to happen for your program to be successful? In other words, how many people need to be served by a program?

   ____

   ____

   ____

3. When do you want this to happen? By what specific date?

   ____

   ____

   ____

Now Write Your Objectives

Use the information in your answers above to write statements of your objectives for each key result area.

Objective 1: ______________________________

____

____

Objective 2: ______________________________

____

____

Objective 3: ______________________________

____

____

Test Your Objectives

Now test each statement using the following criteria:

Is each statement relevant to the basic purpose of your organization?

1. ____________________
2. ____________________
3. ____________________

Is each statement practical?

1. ____________________
2. ____________________
3. ____________________

Does each statement provide a challenge?

1. ____________________
2. ____________________
3. ____________________

Is each stated in objectively measurable terms?

1. ____________________
2. ____________________
3. ____________________

Do you have a specific date for completion?

1. ____________________
2. ____________________
3. ____________________

Does each statement contribute to a balance of activites in line with your HCO's strengths and weaknesses?

1. ____________________
2. ____________________
3. ____________________

Chapter 6

Developing Strategy and Operational Plans

To mean well is nothing without to do well.

Plautus
Trinummus

What people say you cannot do, you try and find that you can.

Henry David Thoreau

To be a success in business, be daring, be first, be different.

Henry Marchant

After developing a set of objectives for the time period covered by the strategic plan, the strategy necessary for accomplishing those objectives must be formulated. First, an overall strategy must be designed. Then the operating details of that strategy as it relates to providing services, promoting operations, determining location, and increasing revenue sources must be planned to guide the HCO's efforts. This chapter introduces the concept of strategy, and describes strategy elements and approaches to strategy development.

STRATEGY CONCEPTS

The word *strategy* has been used in a number of ways over the years and especially so in the context of business. As we discussed in Chapter 2, strategy means leadership and may be defined as the course of action taken by an organization to achieve its objectives. It is a description first in general terms and then, in increasingly greater detail, of the activities the organization will undertake to meet its goals and fulfill its ongoing mission. Strategy is the catalyst or dynamic element of managing that enables a company to accomplish its objectives.

Strategy development is both a science and an art, a product of both logic and creativity. The scientific aspect deals with assembling and allocating the resources necessary to achieve an organization's objectives with emphasis on matching organizational strengths with environmental opportunities, while working within cost and time constraints. The art of strategy is mainly concerned with the effective utilization of resources, including motivating people to make the strategy work, while being sensitive to the environmental forces that may affect the organization's performance and maintaining the ability to adapt the HCO to these changing conditions.

ALTERNATIVE STRATEGIES

Strategy options are the alternative courses of action evaluated by management before a commitment is made to a specific course of action eventually outlined in the strategic plan. Thus, strategy is the link between objectives and results.

For the most part, there have been two basic strategies an HCO could use to accomplish its objectives. These are a differentiation strategy and a focus strategy. Now, however, with pressures from payers and competitors forcing emphasis on cost containment in delivery of health services, a third basic competitive strategy is a necessary consideration: cost leadership. In any case, the strategy selected must be an outgrowth of the organization's basic mission or purpose. Let's briefly review the different strategies.

Differentiation Strategy

A differentiation strategy concentrates on developing and delivering products or services that stand out in the client's mind as distinct from those of other HCOs. HCOs that pursue this strategy see that an important aspect of being able to fulfill their missions involves cultivating the perception of uniqueness in the minds of their service recipients and sponsors regarding the HCO's services or products. In a sense this means building "brand loyalty," so that when patients or potential patients think of a certain service their first thought includes the HCO.

For many HCOs, a differentiation strategy takes the form of several distinct services, each targeted to meet specific needs of patient groups in the HCO's service area. For instance, a medical group practice originally specializing in orthopedic services could consider an expansion in programs offered.

The group might seek to set itself apart from its peers in the eyes of patients by offering natural extensions of its current operations. Physical therapy, outpatient rehabilitative medicine, or sports medicine services could be added to the practice as part of a continuum of services for its patients. The patients would benefit from the close coordination of services and the convenience of multiple services under one roof. The medical group practice would benefit from multiple additional sources of revenue.

By developing a reputation for high quality in programs such as these, an HCO can come to be associated in a positive way with certain types of needs for a broad cross section of the community. Becoming synonymous with quality services in the public's mind can enhance the diversity and intensity of sources of revenue generation. The end result of such differentiation is a greater capability to fulfill the HCO's mission mandate in terms of its patient/client needs.

Focus Strategy

Another basic approach an HCO can use to pursue its objectives is a focus strategy. A focus strategy concentrates on a single service or category of very similar services that meet the needs of a specific group of patients/clients.

The Recreation Center for the Physically Limited (whose mission statement appears in Chapter 3) employs a focus strategy. The Center's services are highly specialized. It focuses on providing recreational activities as a means of enhancing the growth and well-being of its clients.

The Center's service recipients are tightly defined as well. Recreational opportunities are provided for the physically handicapped, excluding children under the age of five, within its service area. Using a focus strategy, the Recreation Center seeks to fill a service gap for the physically challenged in its community.

The main advantages of this strategy are: (1) it capitalizes on the distinctive competencies of the people involved; and (2) it concentrates on doing one thing well. These advantages can also create a knowledge base of how to carry out certain types of programs and can improve efficiency in performing the services.

Cost Leadership

Still another fundamental method for achieving objectives is a cost leadership strategy. The hallmark of this strategy is a major emphasis on efficiency. By keeping costs lowest among providers in the HCO's target region, the organization is effectively positioned to attract and maintain service recipients on the basis of low pricing. The HCO is also better positioned to match other providers' pricing strategies for extended periods as competitive bidding for major contracts becomes a way of life in a managed care industry environment.

Using a cost leadership strategy can be challenging. Since the HCO is competing basically on price, the organization must have a clear understanding of its costs for rendering service. Administrative and indirect costs must be kept to a minimum. Services offered focus more on the fundamentals and less on the frills. In the face of price competition, differences between costs and revenues, or margins, are typically reduced with this strategy, making higher volumes necessary to maintain operating surpluses. All this requires an excellent management information system to track actual costs of care and revenues generated.

Some of these cost leadership operational demands, such as large service volumes, are beyond the capabilities of many stand-alone HCOs, however. They sometimes require integrated relationships with other providers, either with peers (horizontal integration) or with organizations that provide other spectrums of care (vertical integration).

Horizontal integration strategies take the form of alliances between providers of similar services, such as hospital groups. Vertical integration refers to the major addition of services closer to the client (forward vertical integration), as when a nursing home decides to add home health services. It may also mean backward vertical integration, where the added services move away from the patient toward suppliers, as in the case of a large regional hospital that contracts management services out to a small rural hospital, hoping to draw patient referrals requiring more sophisticated treatment.

To achieve these integrated relationships, there are a number of implementation strategies available. These include strategic alliances, joint ventures, and mergers.

Strategic Alliances

These are loose relationships among providers to achieve certain common goals. While contractual relationships are common, there is no exchange of ownership or loss of ultimate local autonomy. The organizations combining forces typically are not directly in competition with one another within a region.

Strategic alliances seek some of the economies of scale required by the cost leadership strategy by, for instance, standardizing certain aspects of their operations and combining their purchasing power. These moves provide added negotiating clout with suppliers of equipment and materials as well as with suppliers of specialized consulting and health program services. One such alliance is the Voluntary Hospitals of America (VHA). VHA member facilities enjoy such benefits as purchasing discounts, access to consultants on operational issues, and architectural services, among others.

Joint Ventures

These are more formalized versions of strategic alliances where two HCOs seek in various ways to combine strengths and overcome the weaknesses of their respective organizations, often with some exchange or pooling of management control of the venture. HMOs are a prime example of this technique. Physician groups and hospitals combine forces, allowing the medical groups to better compete on a price basis where services and risks are spread over larger, combined patient volumes. The hospitals benefit by solidifying their patient referrals and by gaining additional control over the costs of care. In this vertical relationship, both entities are better positioned to bid competitively for the health services of large employee groups.

Mergers

These arrangements take the joint venture a major step further. Here, as in the joint venture, two organizations seek to do better together what they had been doing by going it alone. With the merger, however, the separate organizations become a single entity through some exchange of ownership. Typically the conditions driving such a major ownership change portend dramatic, often negative, consequences if ignored. Market share, profitability, and organizational viability are often threatened without some major operational changes.

By combining resources and ownership, the HCOs hope to accomplish such things as greater efficiency through reduction in service duplication, improved and enlarged geographic coverage, larger volumes of care, and improvements in other critical operational aspects. An example is Health Net and Qual-Med's $775 million merger in 1993.[1] Their combining of resources produced California's largest proprietary managed care organization, with 1.1 million enrollees.

Despite these potential benefits, successful mergers are difficult to achieve. Autonomy and managerial control are not given away lightly. But even where this transition is successfully negotiated, mergers often run afoul of the differences in organizational cultures between the merging partners. The differences can be so profound and the personalities of the organizations so entrenched that mergers have failed to achieve anticipated results on this basis alone.

Using a cost leadership strategy in an environment dominated more and more by managed care means partnering among service providers. The higher overhead of stand-alone organizations, the substantial financial risks of mistakes in capitation expense and revenue estimates in making competitive bids, and the bargaining power with clients and suppliers of larger competitor groups make it very difficult for individual providers to effectively implement a cost/price leadership approach by themselves. Alliances, joint ventures, or mergers can provide a means for maintaining organizational viability in a fast-changing healthcare environment.

Tactical Issues

The number of employees covered by employer healthcare plans using managed care arrangements has almost doubled since 1988, to over half of all employees covered.[2] Some estimates are that by the year 2000, as much as 65 percent of the U.S. population will be covered by managed care plans.[3] Because of this growth, a closer look at some special concerns in pursuing participation in a managed care network is warranted.

Managed care networks fundamentally exist to drive down healthcare costs for large employers, consortiums of employers, and other groups capable of wielding enough buying power to engage the interests of health service providers. Most providers do not control enough service assets to compete alone in this new environment. As evidence, over 75 percent of physicians, a provider category known for its preference for delivery autonomy, have become participants in managed care plans.[4] This constraint typically means that providers must look to contracting with other providers or a managed care company to compete.

Gary Scott Davis points to some special concerns on which providers should focus in striking a managed care alliance.[5] First, your HCO should have all its critical constituencies in agreement to enter into a managed care arrangement. Feeling competitive pressures, some hospitals have tried to move into such arrangements without having the support of its medical staff, with abortive consequences.

Second, since your HCO is seeking some safety in joining with multiple providers, care should be taken that risk is actually shared through the contractual mechanisms of the managed care company. Your HCO should have a clear understanding of how its budget with the managed care company will be handled in relation to other providers' budgets. Budget surpluses and deficits across participants should be shared through the managed care company's utilization management procedures.

Third, the track record of your managed care company should be investigated. Word of mouth is a good start. But also check for any operational changes recently required by regulatory agencies. Also note the firm's size and growth. The firm should have a substantial portion of your target market, at least 10 percent, to indicate its staying power.

Fourth, check on the utilization requirements for plan participants before finalizing financial agreements. Your plans for making up lost income from some heavily discounted services with revenues from other services with higher margins can be at risk. Some managed care companies have policies referring patients only to designated facilities for these services. These facilities may be lower-cost providers within the managed care network.

Fifth, avoid contract clauses with 60- to 90-day termination notices when your intent is for a long-term contract. Since managed care networks are out to save money, in short order they may drop certain providers who are not the least costly. All your work at estimating your costs and negotiating on the merits toward a long-term relationship may go for naught with such escape clauses.

Entering into managed care agreements can be an essential method of stabilizing income sources for many HCOs. For the agreements to work, however, there must be substantial and equitable vested interests for all participants, so that the organizations are committed and fully engaged in the alliance. An example is Mississippi Health Partners, a physician-hospital alliance involving three hospitals and approximately 350 physicians. The hospitals put up 50 percent of the roughly $1 million in seed money to establish the alliance. Approximately 100 primary care physicians invested $1,100 apiece, and another 200 specialists put up $1,500 each, to match the hospitals' contributions. The organization uses two types of voting stock, with the physicians holding ten votes of each and the hospitals six of each. Board decisions are determined by a simple majority of each type of stock.[6]

FACTORS INFLUENCING STRATEGY SELECTION

At least four factors influence the choice of a strategy selected by the organization: its internal resources, the distinctive competencies of its leaders and staff, its stage in its life cycle, and strategies used by competing HCOs. There is no one best strategy that will always prove successful. Instead, the strategy that is chosen must be the one that is best for the HCO, given the nature of these four factors. Resources, for example, may limit the organization to a focus strategy. The organization may even be an innovator in terms of ideas but not have the financial, communication, or personnel resources to offer other services.

As emphasized in Chapter 2, an HCO's strategy must be derived from its organizational purpose and objectives. If the organizational mission is focused on serving needs of diverse groups, the strategy used must be one that is compatible. In other words, what an organization *does* must be a function of what it *is*.

The distinctive competencies of an HCO have a direct bearing on the strategy selected. Distinctive skills and experience in dealing with the physically challenged, for example, can influence strategy choice. These distinctive competencies are the basis of doing things well.

The organization's life-cycle stage is an additional factor influencing strategy selection. For example, an organization may begin with a focus strategy but over time add programs that serve more varied needs. Repositioning the organization through introducing new programs or serving new markets would be a pivotal point in reformulating strategy. The strategy selected must be given sufficient time to be implemented and affect groups served, but an obviously ineffective strategy should be changed. This concept should be understood without mention, but the resistance to change in many organizations is a common phenomenon.

OPERATIONAL PLANS

After all the steps have been taken and a strategy has been developed to meet your objectives and goals, it is time to develop an operational or action plan. The operational plan is the "action" or "doing" stage. Here you serve, hire, fire, build, advertise, and so on. How many times has a group of people planned something and gotten enthusiastic and then nothing happened? This is usually because they did not complete an operational or action plan to implement their strategy.

Operational plans need to be developed in all the areas that are used to support the overall strategy. These include service delivery operations, communications, staffing, and finances. Each of these more detailed plans is designed to spell out what needs to happen in a given area to implement the strategic plan.

The operations plan identifies exactly what services will be provided to a specific group and the exact nature of those services. For example, a home healthcare agency pursuing a differentiation strategy by expanding services must now face up to specifying the limits of the new offerings. Will the expanded services include rehabilitation, or possibly hospice care using volunteers? Perhaps elder care will be offered or equipment rental services will be added in-house instead of contracted for.

The communications plan is used to communicate the nature, location, and time parameters of the program to the intended audience and also to the rest of the HCO's staff. This plan also needs to be well thought-out and carefully analyzed to avoid miscommunication or a lack of communication.

For example, in developing its operations plan, a community rehabilitation center would need a communications strategy to provide information to people about its purpose and services. Its communication strategy could involve three key elements: informing, persuading, and reminding.

1. Informing–This involves providing information to individuals and groups about the organization. Specific elements of this plan call for:

    a. Use of videocassette presentations
    b. Newsletters, pamphlets
    c. Personal speaking appearances by executives or healthcare professionals
    d. Hosting luncheons/educational events
    e. On-site visits by individuals/groups to the HCO's

2. Persuading–This involves presenting the challenges and the benefits of rehabilitation, methods for dealing with these issues, and how the HCO's services deliver on these issues.

    a. Prepare application forms with which service recipients may request additional information or interested individuals may apply as volunteers.

   b. Provide convenient means for patients to access services such as transportation services if there is a major need unfilled in this area.

3. Reminding–This aspect of the strategy is to continue to provide information to people already familiar with the HCO so they will be constantly reminded of its service capabilities.
   a. Send letters/newsletters and other materials regularly.
   b. Develop a complete file of individuals and organizations by name for the future.

The staffing plan deals with identifying who will carry out the activities involved. Since many HCOs must rely on professionals to carry out plans, it may be necessary to develop a recruitment plan just to staff the activity. Such a plan should consider these basic questions. What healthcare professionals will be needed to deliver the services proposed? Can part-time staff or possibly independent contractors be used? If temporaries are to be used, what is the availability of properly credentialed staff in this category?

Finances must also be planned. This is usually done in the form of a financial budget. The budget is the means to execute the plan. If the financial means to support the plan are not available, you must adjust the objectives. There is a constant interplay between the budget and the plan.

Many people do not understand the budgeting process. The budget is a "tool." Too often, however, the budget becomes the tail wagging the dog for the HCO. "We budgeted it so we had better spend it" or "We had better add a little to this year's budget" are statements that reflect this misunderstanding.

Budget money must be tied directly to performance. Performance is measured against objectives. Key results and objectives in an HCO's operation need to be prioritized. Money and resources are then allocated.

An example of this interplay can be reflected in this hypothetical give-and-take regarding the operation of a rehabilitation center. In a planning meeting, the center's leadership confronts the realization that most of their resources for the next two years will have to go into finishing current building programs. Only enough money is available to maintain the staffing status quo even though they want to expand it. That does not mean that appropriate staffing levels are not important–they are. But the timing for expansion and growth for the program cannot come until the other projects are completed.

Shown in Exhibits 6.1 and 6.2 are action plans for a large professional pharmacists' group, with several different types of services and locations planned. The operational or action plans in this example are related directly to the strategy to be used and the objectives to be accomplished in a step-by-step fashion. This forces the planner to align objectives, strategies, and action plans together. Notice that the action plan format takes one objective out of a five-year strategic plan and isolates it for further study and analysis. In this case it shows the targets this professional pharmacists' group is aiming toward in terms of pharmacy operations and professional staff. Definitive efforts should be made to ensure that the targets are clear and understood by everyone prior to action. It is important that all those who execute these plans be in on the planning and be aware of what is going on. That is the key to enthusiasm and support by the staff.

With targets/objectives/goals in mind, the various strategies are agreed upon. They are listed immediately under the objectives. Next, all the actions that must take place must be listed. Also note that there is a section to write in who is in charge, date started, and date completed. This document becomes not only a guide to action but a time line for starting and completing plans.

The person or persons responsible and the expected date of completion must be agreed upon. Every person involved gets a copy of the plan with his/her areas of responsibility marked. Now one person can coordinate a multitude of projects and programs, because there is a clear record of what is to be done. As each action or task is completed, the person responsible sends in a completion report. The coordinator knows what is going on all the time with this approach.

Periodic updates of the action plan are carried out so that everyone sees the progress. After people become accustomed to using the action plan format, they discipline themselves. They do not want others to see that they are falling behind. This is a great timesaving and coordination format. Appendix B presents sample strategic plans to illustrate the development of strategies to accomplish a mission.

Exhibit 6.1
Action Plan: New Pharmacies

OBJECTIVE:
To open 7 new pharmacies within the next five years (1996-2000).
Cumulatively:

1996: 1 pharmacies
1997: 2 pharmacies
1998: 3 pharmacies
1999: 5 pharmacies
2000: 7 pharmacies

STRATEGIES:

A. Explore financing options.
B. Hire marketing consulting firm to determine feasible locations.
C. Select an architect.
D. Select a realtor.

ACTION PLAN	PERSON RESPONSIBLE	START DATE	DATE COMPLETED
Contact 4-5 lending institutions for loan potential and costs.			
Network within professional association for marketing consultants and architect candidates.			
Set up architectural plan review team.			
Establish relationship with realtor.			

SUMMARY

A well-thought-out plan with suggestions from everyone succeeds. How many times do you see HCOs trying to do everything at once? The word "strategic" in the title of this book implies thinking, planning, and seeking order. All this can happen if an action plan coordinates and supports the overall plan.

Exhibit 6.2
Action Plan: Recruiting Pharmacists

OBJECTIVE:
To recruit 50 additional pharmacists in the next five years (1996-2000) for placement at our new locations.
Cumulatively:
1996: 6 pharmacists
1997: 16 pharmacists
1998: 26 pharmacists
1999: 38 pharmacists
2000: 50 pharmacists

STRATEGIES:
A. Make contact with pharmacist program at nearby university to determine recruiting potential and procedures.
B. Develop informational/marketing brochure on current and planned operations for use as a recruiting tool.

ACTION PLAN	PERSON RESPONSIBLE	START DATE	DATE COMPLETED
The assistant administrator will serve as the primary recruiter. The administrator will appoint a selection team to review and recommend candidates to the group's principals who have been screened by the primary recruiter. The assistant administrator will set goals for the number of organizations to be contacted to become part of the placement network.			

REFERENCES

1. "1993–A Boom Year for Healthcare Mergers and Acquisitions." *Modern Healthcare,* 1993, Vol. 23, No. 48, p. 6.

2. Gable, J., D. Lisbon, G. Jonson, and J. Marsteller. "The Health Insurance Picture in 1993: Some Rare Good News." *Health Affiliations* (Millwood), 1994, Vol. 13, No. 1, pp. 327-336.

3. Weiner, J. P. "Forecasting the Effects of Health Reform on U.S. Physician Workforce Requirements: Evidence from HMO Staffing Patterns." *Journal of the American Medical Association,* 1994, Vol. 272, pp. 222-230.

4. Emmons, D. W. and C. J. Simon. *Physician Marketplace Report: Recent Trends in Managed Care*. Chicago: American Medical Association, 1993.

5. Davis, Gary Scott. Cited in Hudson, Terese. "Providers Beware: Managed Care Contracts Can Be Tricky." *Hospitals and Health Networks* (February 5, 1994), p. 72.

6. Kenkel, Paul J. "Physician-Hospital Collaborations Increase, Work to Capture Managed-Care Contracts." *Modern Healthcare* (April 4, 1994), pp. 59-65.

STRATEGY DEVELOPMENT WORKSHEET

This worksheet is provided to help you develop a strategy for your healthcare organization.

Answer These Questions First

1. What are the distinctive competencies of your HCO? What do you do well that makes you different from other HCOs?

   ____

   ____

   ____

2. What market segment or segments should you select to match your organization's skills and resources, and your constituents' needs in those segments?

   ____

   ____

   ____

3. Do you have the skills/resources to pursue several segments or should you concentrate on one segment? Is the revenue potential for that segment large enough to sustain your organization and allow for growth?

   ____

   ____

   ____

Now Develop Your Positioning Statement

1. Distinctive Competencies ______________________________

   ____

   ____

2. Patient/Client Segments Sought ______________________________

   ____

   ____

3. Services to be Offered ______________________________

   ____

   ____

4. Need/Demand for Services ______________________________

____

____

5. Revenue-Generating Potential ____________________________

____

____

6. Growth Potential ____________________________________

____

____

Next develop your overall strategy (Growth, Stability, Retrenchment) for each major program:

Growth (Add or expand spectrum of programs)

Growth: Alternative Strategy 1
Pros
1. ____
2. ____
3. ____
Cons
1. ____
2. ____
3. ____

Growth: Alternative Strategy 2
Pros
1. ____
2. ____
3. ____
Cons
1. ____
2. ____
3. ____

Stability (Keep same programs while improving on effectiveness and efficiency)

Stability: Alternative Strategy 1
Pros
1. ____________________
2. ____________________
3. ____________________

Cons
1. ____________________
2. ____________________
3. ____________________

Stability: Alternative Strategy 2
Pros
1. ____________________
2. ____________________
3. ____________________

Cons
1. ____________________
2. ____________________
3. ____________________

Retrenchment (Major reduction or elimination in existing programs or locations)

Retrenchment: Alternative Strategy 1
Pros
1. ____________________
2. ____________________
3. ____________________

Cons
1. ____________________
2. ____________________
3. ____________________

Retrenchment: Alternative Strategy 2
Pros
1. ____________________
2. ____________________
3. ____________________
Cons
1. ____________________
2. ____________________
3. ____________________

Recommended overall strategy for each program

Justification: Explain why this is the best alternative.
Pros
1. ____________________
2. ____________________
3. ____________________
Cons
1. ____________________
2. ____________________
3. ____________________

Finally, establish operational strategies for each key result area objective in each major program that supports your overall strategy for that program.

An action plan for each key result area should be developed. The action plan establishes coordinated linkages among objectives, strategies, and operational plans and helps you develop the interrelationships among plans at each organizational level. It helps goals come to life with appropriate action.

ACTION PLAN

OBJECTIVE: ____________________

____

____

____

____

____

____

STRATEGIES:

A.____

____

____

B.____

____

____

C.____

____

____

D.____

____

____

E.____

____

____

Action Plan	Person Responsible	Date Started	Date Completed

Chapter 7

Evaluation and Control Procedures

It is a bad plan that admits no modification.

Publilius Syrus
Maxims

Which of you, intending to build a tower, sitteth not down first and counteth the cost?

Luke 14:28

What gets measured gets done.

Mason Haire

The evaluation and control stage of the strategic planning process can be compared to setting out on a journey with a road map. The process includes identifying your destination (objective), determining the best route to your destination (strategy), and then departing for your trip (implementation of your strategy).

During the journey, you look for highway signs (feedback) to tell you if you are on the way to your objective. Signs along the way quickly reveal if you have made a wrong turn and, if so, how you can alter your course to get back on the right road. When you reach your destination, a new route (strategy) may be needed to get you to a new destination.

Imagine what would happen if there were no road signs during your trip to let you know if you were on the right road. It might be too late to continue the trip by the time you realized you were traveling in the wrong direction. Yet, many healthcare organizations are involved in a similar situation, failing to analyze results to determine if objectives are being accomplished.

Failure to establish procedures to appraise and control the strategic plan can lead to less than optimal performance. Many organizations fail to understand the importance of establishing procedures to appraise and control the planning process. This chapter reviews the need for evaluation and control, explains what is to be controlled, and offers some control procedures. Evaluation and control should be a natural follow-through in developing a plan as discussed in Chapter 2. No plan should be considered complete until controls are identified, and the procedures for recording control information and transmitting it to administrators of the plan are established.

INTEGRATION OF PLANNING AND CONTROL

Planning and control should be integral processes. In fact, we view planning as a process that relies on a system for feedback of results. This feedback reflects the organization's performance in reaching its objectives through implementation of the strategic plan. The relationship between planning and control is depicted in Exhibit 7.1.

The strategic planning process results in a strategic plan. This plan is implemented (activities are performed in the manner described in the plan) and results are produced. These results include such things as services rendered, revenue generated, and accompanying constituent attitudes, preferences, and behaviors. Information on these results and other key result areas is given to management, who compare the results with objectives to evaluate performance. This performance evaluation identifies the areas where decisions must be made to adjust activities, people, or finances. The actual decision making controls the plan by altering it to accomplish stated objectives, and a new cycle begins. The information flows are the key to a good control system.

Exhibit 7.1
The Planning and Control Process

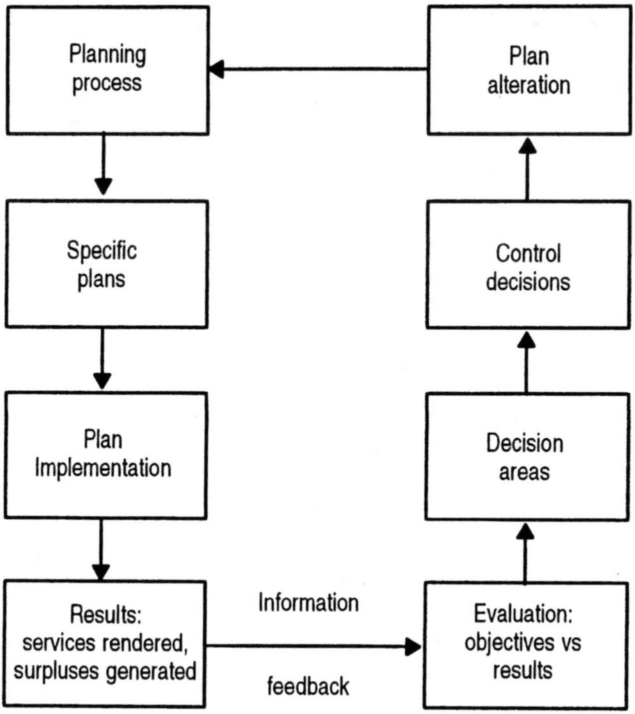

The last stage of the strategic planning process, then, is to review the HCO within each of its divisions to determine if all objectives have been met:

- Have the measurable objectives and goals been accomplished?
- How far did actual performance miss the mark?
- Did the attainment of the objectives and goals in fact support the overall purpose?
- Has the environment changed enough to change the objectives and goals?
- Have additional weaknesses been revealed that will influence changing the objectives of the organization?

- Have additional strengths been added or has your position improved sufficiently to influence the changing of your objectives?
- Has the HCO provided its members with organizational rewards, both extrinsic and intrinsic?
- Is there a feedback system to help members satisfy their high-level needs?

Timing of Information Flows

The strategic plan is supported by operational plans. We plan for the long run but must operate in the short run. Properly controlled operational (short-term) plans result in effective strategic (long-term) plans. The HCO's administration cannot afford to wait for the time period of a plan to pass before control information is available. The information must be available within a time frame that is long enough to allow results to accrue, but short enough to allow actions to align results with objectives.

Although some types of organizations may find weekly or biweekly results necessary, most organizations can adequately control operations with monthly or quarterly reports. Cumulative monthly or quarterly reports become annual reports, which in turn become the feedback needed to control the plan. Deciding what information is provided to which administrators in what time periods is the essence of a control system.

PERFORMANCE EVALUATION AND CONTROL

Performance should be evaluated in many areas to provide a complete analysis of what the results are and what caused them. Three key control areas are services rendered, revenues generated, and patients'/clients' attitudes. Objectives should have been established in all of these areas for the strategic plan.

Services Rendered Control

Control data should be developed on key aspects of the HCO's operations, especially as they relate to major service categories. An example of the type of performance reports a hypothetical home health service could use is shown in Exhibit 7.2, where the numbers of home health visits projected for four areas of professional service are displayed. When such a format is used, the home visits objectives stated in the plan can be broken down on a quarterly basis and become the standard against which actual visits are compared.

Number and percentage variations are calculated, because in some instances a small percentage can result in a large number variation.

A performance index can be calculated by dividing actual participation by the participation objective. Index numbers near 1.00 indicate that expected and actual performance are about equal. Numbers larger than 1.00 indicate above-expected performance, and numbers below 1.00 reveal below-expected performance. Index numbers are especially useful when a large number of programs are involved, because they enable management to identify those programs that need immediate attention.

Revenue/Cost Controls

Several tools are available for establishing cost control procedures, including budgets, expense ratios, and activity costs analysis. Budgets are a common tool used by many organizations for both planning and control. The budget is often established by using historical percentages of various expenses as a percentage of revenues.

Exhibit 7.2
Home Health Visits Report: Quarter 1 (by Professional Area)

Program	(A) Projected Visits	(B) Actual Visits	(C) (B-A) Variation	(D) (C÷A) % Variation	(E) (B÷A) Performance Index
RNs	250.	285.	+ 35.	+ 14.0	1.14
LPNs	425.	465.	+ 40.	+ 9.4	1.09
NAs	640.	518.	- 122.	- 19.1	.81
PTs	200.	203.	+ 3.	+ 1.5	1.02

Thus, once the total level of expected revenues is established, expense items can be budgeted as a percent of total revenue.

If zero-based budgeting is used, where each period's budget is developed from scratch without benefit of the previous period's budget, the objectives to be accomplished must be specified and the expenditures necessary to accomplish these objectives estimated. The estimates become the budgeted expenses for the time period.

Revenues are monitored by tracing charges on a periodic basis, usually at least monthly. A prerequisite to monitoring and evaluating revenue generation is an annual projection of operating expenses. This projection, broken down on a quarterly or monthly basis, becomes the standard from which deviations are analyzed.

For example, an HCO with a projected budget of $1,500,000 for the next fiscal year would be expecting about $375,000 per quarter, or $125,000 per month. However, if there are large variations related to certain times of the year, the variations can be analyzed to determine the proportion of the budgeted amount anticipated per time period. Say, historically, 20 percent of the revenues are generated during January and February each year. Then, instead of budgeting for next year an equal amount for each month in the fiscal year, this percentage can be allocated as the standard for these two months, with the remaining 80 percent allocated across the other ten months of the year.

The same type of analysis used to monitor services rendered (such as the home healthcare visits shown in Exhibit 7.2) can be used to analyze data on revenues. This type of analysis should be performed on a timely basis to enable expansion or cutbacks of programs when revenue levels go above or below the expected amounts for the period.

Once the budget is established, expense variance analysis by line item or expenditure category is used to control costs. A typical procedure is to prepare monthly or quarterly budget reports showing the amount budgeted for the time period and the dollar and percentage variation from the budgeted amount, if any, that exists. Expenditure patterns that vary from the budgeted amounts are then analyzed to determine why the variations occurred.

Another control tool involves the use of financial ratios. The following ratios can be used to make comparisons against established objectives in each category, prior year's ratio performance, and typical ratios for the industry.[1]

Liquidity Ratios
- Cash Ratio (cash and cash equivalents/current liabilities)
- Current Ratio (current assets/current liabilities)
- Asset Ratio (current assets/total assets)

Contribution Ratio
- Donation Ratio (total donations/total revenue)

Return Ratio
- Return on Assets Ratio (total revenue/total assets)

Debt Ratio
- Debt-to-Assets Ratio (total liabilities/total assets)

Operating Ratios
- Net Operating Ratio (excess of income over expenses/total expenses)
- Fund Balance Reserve Ratio (total fund balance/total expenses)
- Cash Reserve Ratio (total cash/total expenses)
- Program Expense Ratio (total program expenses/total expenses)
- Support Services Ratio (total support services expenses/total expenses)

Other Measurements
- Net Surplus or Deficiency (total income less total expenses)

Larger HCOs find revenue/expense centers a useful tool in control. For example, a rehabilitation program might generate revenues through the sale of educational tapes and would incur costs in recording, duplicating, and mailing out tapes, plus overhead and labor costs. Tracking these revenues and expenses in a cost center would help control this service by letting management know if it is operating at breakeven or if it is generating excess revenues that could lead to expanding the service, lowering the price of the tapes, or using the surplus for other services.

Patient/Client Feedback

The final area of performance evaluation concerns your constituents–your patients or clients. This analysis involves an examination of the awareness, knowledge, attitudes, and behaviors of your service recipients. Every organization should want its constituents to become aware of its programs, services, or special personnel capabilities; to possess certain knowledge about its services as they relate to the constituents' specific needs; and to exhibit favorable attitudes and behaviors as recipients of these services. If these factors are specified, as they should be, in the statements of objectives, these objectives become the standards against which current constituent data can be compared.

Data on constituents must be collected on a regular basis. There are many ways to collect data, but annual surveys are commonly used. Constituent data are especially valuable if collected over a long period of time, because awareness levels, satisfaction, attitudes, and behavior can be analyzed to reveal trends and areas for further investigation.

ESTABLISHING PROCEDURES

It should be pointed out that none of the performance evaluation data described are going to be available unless they are required by management and funds are made available to finance data collection methodologies. Thus, data-collecting and -reporting procedures must be set up by the administrators who are going to use the control data in decision making.

The procedures will usually change over time as new types of analysis or reporting methods are found to be better than others. The most important requirement is that the data meet the needs of administrators in taking corrective actions to control activities that fall short of intended results. With the expanded availability and use of computers by HCOs, much of the procedural work can be computerized.

PERFORMANCE EVALUATION GUIDELINES

Several summary guidelines should be kept in mind when establishing an effective system for performance evaluation:

1. Performance evaluation must be self-evaluation.
2. Performance evaluation is healthy for performing, growing individuals.
3. Evaluation should use both objective and subjective measures, since much of the work, while still very important, may be difficult to quantify.
4. "No evaluation" is not an option. Exempting certain individuals can suggest favoritism and influence morale negatively.
5. When an evaluation process is perceived as legitimate, fair, and working, people will tend to use it responsibly. When it is not, people may still perform, but they may not feel the burden of responsibility and go the extra mile.
6. Performance evaluation should be a formal process (that is, it should be systematic and documented).

The control system in general should:

1. be linked to strategy.
2. be simple and economical to use.
3. measure both activities and results.
4. flag the exceptions.
5. focus on key success factors, not trivia.
6. be timely.
7. be flexible as strategy changes with environmental demands.
8. be reality-based where written reports are augmented by face-to-face follow-up (the idea behind MBWA–management by wandering around).

It is in the appraisal and control stage that HCOs really begin to see the benefits of the strategic concepts outlined in this book. When people at all levels know the progress being made toward fulfilling the overall plan, it creates a sense of pride, accomplishment, and excitement. Strategic planning will not work well without a review of performance.

SUMMARY

No planning process should be considered complete until appraisal and control procedures have been established. Without such information, it is impossible to manage an HCO's activities with any sense of clarity about what is actually happening in the organization.

Performance evaluation is vital for control decisions. Information tells management what has happened and serves as the basis for any actions needed to control the activities of the organization toward predetermined objectives.

CONCLUSION

The thoughts we have offered throughout this book, we believe, will help make your healthcare organization more effective. In the end, an organization thinking about instituting a strategic planning program should consider the following points:

1. The decision to implement this management philosophy should not be made in haste.
2. To the extent possible, it should receive management support.
3. It is strongly recommended that some type of training session take place in a neutral environment.
4. An outside resource person (consultant) may be needed to get the program started.
5. When applicable, a person from the organization who can take over as the in-house expert should be assigned to work with the consultant.
6. Each organization must find its own way for its people to set objectives.
7. Each organization should come up with its own best method for handling feedback and reviews.
8. Be prepared to expose your management team to new ideas and new ways of approaching managerial problems.
9. Ways should be found to involve all employees in some decision making.
10. Personnel performance reviews must be conducted at regular, scheduled intervals.
11. Be prepared to spend time and hard work keeping the program viable, especially in the first six months.
12. Periodic reviews of strategic plan progress are a must, and must be done by the boss.

13. Every organization and each of its divisions can adapt management by objectives (MBO) to its situation.
14. Goals must be negotiated rather than imposed unilaterally by management.
15. Both extrinsic and intrinsic rewards must be obtainable by the individual and the work team.
16. Use methods for setting, reviewing, and updating MBO that require a minimum of paperwork.
17. If you start using MBO, begin benefiting from its use, and then stop, expect a big drop-off in morale.
18. Don't let a staff department dominate your program.
19. Involve constituents in the planning process through surveys or interviews.

May your HCO's future be a bright one.

REFERENCE

1. Robinson, C. "A Study of the Financial Statement Ratios of ECFA Members: An Executive Overview." Paper presentation, University of San Francisco (January 1990), pp. 2-3.

EVALUATION AND CONTROL WORKSHEET

This worksheet will aid you in developing tools to measure progress toward your HCO's objectives.

Answer the Following Questions

1. What kinds of information do you need to evaluate a program's or service's success?

   ____

   ____

   ____

2. Who should receive and review this information?

   ____

   ____

   ____

3. What time periods do you want to use to analyze the data? Weekly? Monthly?

   ____

   ____

   ____

4. What record-keeping system do you need to devise to make sure the information you want is recorded for the time periods you specified in question 3?

   ____

   ____

   ____

Now Set Up Your Control Procedures

1. Specify the areas to be controlled:

   A. ___________________________________

   B. ___________________________________

   C. ___________________________________

   D. ___________________________________

2. Specify the format of the data for each area. (Is it to be numbers by month by program? Do you want number and percentage variations?)

   A. ____________________

   B. ____________________

   C. ____________________

   D. ____________________

3. Specify how the data are to be collected, who is to collect and analyze the data, and who is to receive the results of the analysis:

   A. How will the data be collected? ____________________

   ____

   ____

   B. Who has responsibility to collect and analyze the data?

   ____

   ____

   ____

   C. Who is to receive which type of analysis?

Administrator	Types of Analysis
1. ____________	1. ____________
2. ____________	2. ____________
3. ____________	3. ____________
4. ____________	4. ____________

APPENDIXES

APPENDIX A: STRATEGIC PLANNING WORKSHEETS AND STRATEGIC PLAN OUTLINE

PLANNING PROCESS WORKSHEET

This worksheet is provided to aid your healthcare organization in starting the strategic planning process. Use the answers to these questions to provide a foundation for completing the remaining worksheets.

1. Who should be involved in the planning process?

____

____

____

2. Where will planning sessions be held?

____

____

____

3. When will planning sessions be held?

____

____

____

4. What types of background material do participants need prior to starting the first session?

____

____

____

5. Who will lead the process? Who will ultimately be responsible for arranging sessions, and getting material typed, reproduced, and distributed?

____

____

____

6. When and how will the staff, board, employees, or others be involved in the process?

____

____

____

7. How will the results be communicated to everyone in the organization?

____

____

____

8. Who will train/supervise managers in working with their own staff and in setting objectives, developing action plans, and conducting performance appraisals?

____

____

____

9. How frequently will the process be reviewed and by whom?

____

____

____

10. Who will be responsible for dealing with external groups (revenue sources, independent healthcare professionals, media, consultants) in preparing the plan?

____

____

____

MISSION AND VISION STATEMENTS WORKSHEET

This worksheet will aid you in writing mission and vision statements for your healthcare organization.

Mission statement

1. Write a statement for the following areas:

   Internal operations statement: ________________________________

   ____

   ____

   ____

   External clientele statement: ________________________________

   ____

   ____

   ____

   Needs served statement: ________________________________

   ____

   ____

   ____

2. Now evaluate the statement.

   Does it define boundaries within which your healthcare organization will operate?

   ____

   ____

   ____

   Does it define the need(s) that your HCO is attempting to meet?

   ____

   ____

   ____

Does it reflect what kind of organization you need to be in order to achieve success in the future?

____

____

____

Do you intend to have local, regional, national, or international scope?

____

____

____

Does it define the market (patients/customers/clientele) that your HCO is reaching?

____

____

____

Has there been input from appropriate organizational members?

____

____

____

Does it include the word "service," or a word with similar meaning?

____

____

____

3. Next, submit it to others familiar with your organization to evaluate your statement of purpose and offer suggestions on improving the statement. In other words, does the statement say to others what you want it to say?

____

____

____

Vision Statement

1. Write statements which answer the following questions:

   What do we want our organization to be like in the future?

   ____

   ____

   ____

   What do we want to be known for in the future?

   ____

   ____

   ____

   In what areas of our operation do we aspire to be the very best?

   ____

   ____

   ____

   What do we want our employees to do in achieving the above?

   ____

   ____

   ____

2. Evaluate the vision statement.

   Are the statements clearly phrased and understandable to all the HCO's employees?

   ____

   ____

   ____

   Are the statements actively phrased in order to generate energy and enthusiasm within the organization?

   ____

   ____

   ____

   Are the statements concise and memorable?

   ____

   ____

   ____

SITUATION ANALYSIS AND ASSUMPTIONS WORKSHEET

This worksheet will aid you in completing a Strengths, Weaknesses, Opportunities, and Threats (SWOT) analysis.

Step 1. **External Environment Analysis:** From industry surveys and your own sources of information, take your organization's pulse. You are looking for trends–what is going on now and how this relates to past trends that have influenced your HCO's performance. From this analysis, list key opportunities and threats for each of the following environmental sectors.

Government

Opportunities

1. ______________________________
2. ______________________________
3. ______________________________

Threats

1. ______________________________
2. ______________________________
3. ______________________________

Economy

Opportunities

1. ______________________________
2. ______________________________
3. ______________________________

Threats

1. ______________________________
2. ______________________________
3. ______________________________

Technology

Opportunities

1. __________
2. __________
3. __________

Threats

1. __________
2. __________
3. __________

Social Trends

Opportunities

1. __________
2. __________
3. __________

Threats

1. __________
2. __________
3. __________

Patients/Clients

Opportunities

1. __________
2. __________
3. __________

Threats

1. __________
2. __________
3. __________

Reimbursement Sources/Sponsorship

Opportunities

1. ______________________________
2. ______________________________
3. ______________________________

Threats

1. ______________________________
2. ______________________________
3. ______________________________

Competing HCOs

Opportunities

1. ______________________________
2. ______________________________
3. ______________________________

Threats

1. ______________________________
2. ______________________________
3. ______________________________

Next, evaluate your external analysis:

Have you listed several international/national trends that affect your HCO?

____

____

____

Have you listed several local trends that affect your HCO?

____

____

____

Have you identified trends unique to your HCO (e.g., availability of certain healthcare professionals)?

____

____

____

Have you listed several of your most important competitors?

____

____

____

Which are growing?______________________________

____

Which are declining?_____________________________

____

What are the successful ones doing?_______________

____

Step 2. **Internal Operations Analysis:** Using the question guides below and your own information, list key strengths and weaknesses for each of the following sectors of your HCO's operations.

Management and Planning Systems

Use these questions to help you prepare your strengths and weaknesses list for this portion of your HCO's operation.

Do you have a planning system?

____

____

____

How does it work?

____

____

____

Is the organizational structure of your HCO allowing effective use of resources?

Is control centralized or decentralized?

Are performance measures and information system controls in evidence? What are they?

What staffing needs do you have?

Is there a motivation problem?

Is your current strategy defined? Is it working?

How efficient are operations?

What is your synopsis of the current management situation?

Now list your strengths and weaknesses for this section of your HCO's operations.

Strengths

Weaknesses

Financial Resources

Use these questions to help you prepare your strengths and weaknesses list for this portion of your HCO's operation.

What is your current financial situation?

Do you have regular financial statements prepared?

What tools would be beneficial in analysis?

Do you have pro forma statements for revenue centers such as rehabilitative care, hospice care, etc.?

____

____

____

Do you have a cash budget?

____

____

____

Do you have a capital budget?

____

____

____

Has a ratio analysis been prepared?

____

____

____

Do you understand the time value of money?

____

____

____

Do you understand and use break-even analysis?

____

____

____

Have you analyzed current financial policies?

____

____

____

Do you have cash policies?

How are accounts receivable analyzed?

How are accounts payable analyzed?

Do you control inventory levels?

Do you have a debt retirement plan?

Give a synopsis of your current financial situation.

Accounting analysis:

Depreciation procedures?

Tax considerations?

Decentralized/centralized operations? ____________________

____

Responsibility accounting? ____________________

____

Tools beneficial in analysis:

Do you have budgets (short- and long-range) established?

____

____

____

Do you perform variance analysis comparing actual against planned performance?

____

____

____

What costing methods are used?

____

____

____

Do you do contribution margin analysis?

____

____

____

Are there adequate controls, especially of cash, for each of your HCO's programs?

____

____

____

What is your synopsis of the current accounting situation?

Now list your strengths and weaknesses for this section of your HCO's operations.

Strengths

Weaknesses

Marketing Resources

Use these questions to help you prepare your strengths and weaknesses list for this portion of your HCO's operation.

Have you established marketing policies?

Have you established what you will and will not do in marketing your services?

Have you identified your patients/clients?

Have you identified your funding/reimbursement sponsors?

____

____

____

What are your competitors' services and products, level of demand, and relative market positions?

____

____

____

What are your distribution systems and location of facilities and how effective are they?

____

____

____

Is your services' price/fee structure current and appropriate?

____

____

____

What promotion (advertising, sales promotion, and personal selling) activities are you using?

____

____

____

What is your synopsis of the current marketing situation?

____

____

____

Now list your strengths and weaknesses for this section of your HCO's operations.

Strengths

____

____

____

Weaknesses

Operations or Services Resources

What are your operations capacities?

What shape are your facilities in?

What is the age and serviceability of your equipment?

How automated are your operations?

What are your transportation capabilities?

Are safety programs adequate?

How effective is your inventory control?

Do you use quality control systems?

Now list your strengths and weaknesses for this section of your HCO's operations.

Strengths

Weaknesses

Next, evaluate the services of your professional staff:

Range of services offered?

Number of services rendered, patients served by service category?

Number and age of professional staff by service category?

____

____

____

Now, evaluate your internal analysis:

Have you listed and analyzed all major internal factors with significant impact on your organization's operations?

____

____

____

Step 3. **<u>Development of Assumptions:</u>** List the major assumptions on which your plan is based.

1._____________________________________

2._____________________________________

3._____________________________________

4._____________________________________

5._____________________________________

OBJECTIVES WORKSHEET

This worksheet will aid you in developing objectives for your HCO's operations.

Answer These Questions First

1. What do your objectives need to relate to–patients, services, revenues, professional staffing, other areas? What about other key result areas?

   ____

   ____

   ____

2. What needs to happen for your program to be successful? In other words, how many people need to be served by a program?

   ____

   ____

   ____

3. When do you want this to happen? By what specific date?

   ____

   ____

   ____

Now Write Your Objectives

Use the information in your answers above to write statements of your objectives for each key result area.

Objective 1: ____

____

____

Objective 2: ____

____

____

Objective 3: ____

____

____

Test Your Objectives

Now test each statement using the following criteria:

Is each statement relevant to the basic purpose of your organization?

1. ____
2. ____
3. ____

Is each statement practical?

1. ____
2. ____
3. ____

Does each statement provide a challenge?

1. ____
2. ____
3. ____

Is each stated in objectively measurable terms?

1. ____
2. ____
3. ____

Do you have a specific date for completion?

1. ____
2. ____
3. ____

Does each statement contribute to a balance of activites in line with your HCO's strengths and weaknesses?

1. ____
2. ____
3. ____

STRATEGY DEVELOPMENT WORKSHEET

This worksheet is provided to help you develop a strategy for your healthcare organization.

Answer These Questions First

1. What are the distinctive competencies of your HCO? What do you do well that makes you different from other HCOs?

   ____

   ____

   ____

2. What market segment or segments should you select to match your organization's skills and resources, and your constituents' needs in those segments?

   ____

   ____

   ____

3. Do you have the skills/resources to pursue several segments or should you concentrate on one segment? Is the revenue potential for that segment large enough to sustain your organization and allow for growth?

   ____

   ____

   ____

Now Develop Your Positioning Statement

1. Distinctive Competencies ________________________

   ____

   ____

2. Patient/Client Segments Sought ____________________

   ____

   ____

3. Services to be Offered __________________________

   ____

   ____

4. Need/Demand for Services ______________________________

____

____

5. Revenue-Generating Potential __________________________

____

____

6. Growth Potential _____________________________________

____

____

Next develop your overall strategy (Growth, Stability, Retrenchment) for each major program:

Growth (Add or expand spectrum of programs)

Growth: Alternative Strategy 1
Pros
1. ____
2. ____
3. ____
Cons
1. ____
2. ____
3. ____

Growth: Alternative Strategy 2
Pros
1. ____
2. ____
3. ____
Cons
1. ____
2. ____
3. ____

Stability (Keep same programs while improving on effectiveness and efficiency)

Stability: Alternative Strategy 1
Pros
1. ______________________________
2. ______________________________
3. ______________________________

Cons
1. ______________________________
2. ______________________________
3. ______________________________

Stability: Alternative Strategy 2
Pros
1. ______________________________
2. ______________________________
3. ______________________________

Cons
1. ______________________________
2. ______________________________
3. ______________________________

Retrenchment (Major reduction or elimination in existing programs or locations)

Retrenchment: Alternative Strategy 1
Pros
1. ______________________________
2. ______________________________
3. ______________________________

Cons
1. ______________________________
2. ______________________________
3. ______________________________

Retrenchment: Alternative Strategy 2

Pros

1. ______

2. ______

3. ______

Cons

1. ______

2. ______

3. ______

Recommended overall strategy for each program

Justification: Explain why this is the best alternative.

Pros

1. ______

2. ______

3. ______

Cons

1. ______

2. ______

3. ______

Finally, establish operational strategies for each key result area objective in each major program that supports your overall strategy for that program.

An action plan for each key result area should be developed. The action plan establishes coordinated linkages among objectives, strategies, and operational plans and helps you develop the interrelationships among plans at each organizational level. It helps goals come to life with appropriate action.

ACTION PLAN

OBJECTIVE: ______

______

______

______

______

______

STRATEGIES:

A. ______________________________

____

____

B. ______________________________

____

____

C. ______________________________

____

____

D. ______________________________

____

____

E. ______________________________

____

____

Action Plan	Person Responsible	Date Started	Date Completed

EVALUATION AND CONTROL WORKSHEET

This worksheet will aid you in developing tools to measure progress toward your HCO's objectives.

Answer the Following Questions

1. What kinds of information do you need to evaluate a program's or service's success?

   ____

   ____

   ____

2. Who should receive and review this information?

   ____

   ____

   ____

3. What time periods do you want to use to analyze the data? Weekly? Monthly?

   ____

   ____

   ____

4. What record-keeping system do you need to devise to make sure the information you want is recorded for the time periods you specified in question 3?

   ____

   ____

   ____

Now Set Up Your Control Procedures

1. Specify the areas to be controlled:

   A. ____

   B. ____

   C. ____

   D. ____

2. Specify the format of the data for each area. (Is it to be numbers by month by program? Do you want number and percentage variations?)

   A. ____

   B. ____

   C. ____

   D. ____

3. Specify how the data are to be collected, who is to collect and analyze the data, and who is to receive the results of the analysis:

   A. How will the data be collected? ____________________

   ____

   ____

   B. Who has responsibility to collect and analyze the data?

   ____

   ____

   ____

   C. Who is to receive which type of analysis?

Administrator	Types of Analysis
1. ________________	1. ________________
2. ________________	2. ________________
3. ________________	3. ________________
4. ________________	4. ________________

STRATEGIC PLAN OUTLINE

Using the information developed with the strategic planning worksheets, your strategic plan can be compiled. Plan descriptions can take many forms. (Note sample plans.) One useful approach is captured in the following outline.

Strategic Plan

I. Executive Summary
*Highlights of each of the following plan sections (1-2 pages)

II. Mission Statement

III. Overview of Overall Strategies and Strategic Objectives

1. Description of major challenges and problems facing the HCO.
2. Description of major assumptions on which the strategic plan is based.
3. Summary of major objectives and overall strategies as they relate to mission and challenges noted; describe how major strategies:
   a. capitalize on distinctive competence and key strengths
   b. manage around or improve on major weaknesses
   c. overcome major external threats
   d. tap key opportunities
   e. fulfill mission

IV> Strategic Plan Implementation: Operational Objectives and Strategies by Program or Service

1. Program 1
   a. Key results area 1
      1. Major objective 1
         * strategy 1 description to achieve major objective 1
         * strategy 2 description to achieve major objective 1
         * evaluation and control standards and time frames
      2. Major objective 2
         * strategy 1 description to achieve major objective 2
         * strategy 2 description to achieve major objective 2
         * evaluation and control standards and time frames
   b. Key results area 2
      1. Major objective 1
         * strategy 1 description to achieve major objective 1
         * strategy 2 description to achieve major objective 1
         * evaluation and control standards and time frames

2. Major objective 2
    * strategy 1 description to achieve major objective 2
    * strategy 2 description to achieve major objective 2
    * evaluation and control standards and time frames

2. Program 2
    a. Key results area 1
        1. Major objective 1
            * strategy 1 description to achieve major objective 1
            * strategy 2 description to achieve major objective 1
            * evaluation and control standards and time frames
        2. Major objective 2
            * strategy 1 description to achieve major objective 2
            * strategy 2 description to achieve major objective 2
            * evaluation and control standards and time frames
    b. Key results area 2
        1. Major objective 1
            * strategy 1 description to achieve major objective 1
            * strategy 2 description to achieve major objective 1
            * evaluation and control standards and time frames
        2. Major objective 2
            * strategy 1 description to achieve major objective 2
            * strategy 2 description to achieve major objective 2
            * evaluation and control standards and time frames

V. Summary and Conclusion

* Highlights of plan's key points showing how they successfully deal with major issues and problems of the HCO and fulfill ongoing mission.

APPENDIX B: SAMPLE STRATEGIC PLANS

Healthcare Department of a State Penitentiary: Strategic Plan*

I. Statement of Purpose

The Healthcare Department of the State Penitentiary exists to protect the public, the employee, and the offender by providing quality healthcare to offenders.

II. Environmental Analysis

A. The inmate population has increased from 850 inmates in year 1 to 1,484 inmates in September of year 5, and DOC will increase by 901 inmates in fiscal year 6 and 684 inmates in fiscal year 7.
B. The legislature will begin to mandate the minimum sentence an offender can receive for particular offenses.
C. The number of inmates over the age of 65 is increasing due to longer sentences.
D. There is a lack of infirmary beds for long-term-care inmates.
E. The legislature has not increased funding to add bed space in the infirmary.
F. OSHA is mandating more regulations in the healthcare industry to prevent the spread of infectious diseases.
G. Active tuberculosis cases within the prison system have increased.

III. Strengths

A. There is excellent administrative support from the Warden and the Medical Administrator.

---

*This is an actual strategic plan. Information has been disguised to protect the confidentiality of the organization.

B. The employee turnover is low due to long-term benefits of working for the State.
C. There is excellent team spirit shown by staff in helping one another to accomplish the job.
D. The staff is competent and can perform necessary duties with limited available resources.

IV. Weaknesses

A. There is inconsistency in skill and experience levels of Licensed Practical Nurses.
B. Lack of staff–There are nine FTE (full-time equivalent) positions that have been unfillable for over two years.
C. Handicap facilities are limited in the medical unit for dealing with elderly and disabled inmates–i.e., shower, tub, etc.
D. There are no OSHA-mandated isolation cells for infectious disease containment.
E. The communication between Administration and Department of Corrections staff is inconsistent.
F. Funding is lacking for needed equipment, education, and facilities.

V. Assumptions

A. The inmate population will continue to increase by approximately 200 inmates per year.
B. Funding by the legislature will not increase enough to ease overcrowding.
C. Inmates will demand more than basic-quality care.
D. Long-term-care inmates will jam the DOC infirmary beds, preventing the care of acutely ill inmates.
E. The "Supervised Pre-Parole Release" program will be repealed.
F. The Department of Corrections will again be put under the control of the federal court system.

VI. Goals, Objectives, and Strategies

A. Improve staffing level by the end of fiscal year year 6.
   1. Realign FTEs into fillable positions.

2. Recruit employees from medical schools.

B. Decrease inmate grievances/lawsuits 10 percent by July year 6.
   1. Emphasize to staff the necessity to meet inmate needs in a timely manner.
   2. Review all requests of staff answered by other medical persons.

C. Maintain overtime pay at 5 percent or less for the next 12 months.
   1. Confer with employees not completing their duties within the shift.
   2. Correctively discipline employees who abuse sick leave.
   3. Provide flexible staffing when possible.

D. Maintain turnover rate at 10 percent or less for the next 12 months.
   1. Hold exit interviews when employees leave.
   2. Emphasize team spirit during staff meetings.

E. Work with the DOC Medical Administrator to expand long-term-care beds.
   1. The three Health Administrators whose facilities contain infirmary beds will develop a strategic plan to present to the DOC Medical Administrator.
   2. Present the requirements necessary to be in compliance with the Americans with Disabilities Act (ADA) and the stipulations of the Justice Department.

F. Develop adequate isolation facilities for tuberculosis and other contagious diseases by the end of fiscal year 6.
   1. Request input from the State Health Department.
   2. Meet with Administration and emphasize the need for immediate compliance.

G. All nurses to be IV- and trauma-certified by December year 6.
   1. Arrange training for IV and trauma schools.
   2. Voice expectations to staff.

H. Productivity will stay between 95 percent and 100 percent.
   1. Continue to cross-train employees.
   2. Use volunteers as much as possible.

VII. Issues and Problems

A. Major.
   1. Lack of staff, with additional duties added to an already stretched staff.
   2. Need for education of staff.

B. Minor.
   1. Lack of time for treating and educating inmates with chronic health problems.
   2. Fixed budget.

VIII. Analysis

A. OSHA standards require much change and adaptation.
B. Cost containment and inmate service are imperative.
C. Overall inmate population is increasing, with a huge increase in long-term care of inmates.
D. Staff is expected to give high-quality care to higher-acuity cases with less resources.
E. Staff is challenged to adapt to a constantly hostile and dangerous work environment.
F. Fewer financial and support resources are available.

IX. Alternative Solutions

A. Education.
   1. Send staff for IV and trauma training.
      Pro: Staff would get solid education.
      Cons: High expense. Staff needed on unit.
   2. Use self-directed education.
      Pros: Learn at own pace. Reference library readily available.
      Cons: Staff wants hands-on learning. Not self-motivated. Personal expense.

B. Lack of staff.
   1. Pay overtime/comp time.
      Pros: Staff could earn extra pay. Productivity standard would be met.

Cons: Staff burnout. Increased overtime percentage and costs. Decreased quality of care.

2. Use volunteers.
   Pros: Decreased staff load. No cost to agency. Non-patient-care activities accomplished more timely.
   Cons: Increased expense of training. DOC guidelines for working with inmates. Volunteers may be less trained than unit staff. Liability. May not be readily available when needed most.
3. Realign FTEs to fillable positions.
   Pros: Two part-time employees could be hired versus one full-time. More frontline staff could be hired. Less expense to department.
   Cons: Part-time employees can work limited amount of hours.
4. Maintain status quo.
   Pros: Budget savings to department. No additional change for staff.
   Cons: No increase in productivity. Will not result in improvements.

X. Recommendations

Realign the available FTE positions we are currently unable to fill into fillable positions to decrease the workload on present staff. Continue to cross-train employees so as to assist others on slow workdays. Provide ample opportunities for continuing education outside the facility.

Work diligently with administrators from the other Department of Corrections infirmaries on a strategic plan proposal to deal with long-term-care inmates.

Medical Clinic: Strategic Plan*

I. Purpose

The purpose of the clinic is to ensure that our customers, both internal and external, receive the services and resources that enhance the delivery of high-quality healthcare to our market area.

The clinic operates in five locations within the local area and must maintain the ability to expand throughout the southern part of the state. The clinic operates as a for-profit entity serving clinic physicians and staff, third-party payers, vendors, the community, and the patient.

The clinic's values integrated into the achievement of purpose are service, performance, integrity, respect, innovation, and teamwork.

II. Environmental Analysis

A. Physician recruitment and retention is expensive and competitive. The local market has seen an increasing demand for primary care physicians that has resulted in yearly increases in cost of new physicians. The current base rate for a new primary care physician is $110,000 plus school loan repayment, moving expenses, sometimes signing bonuses, and the usual benefit package that includes health, disability, life, and liability insurance, vacation, CME (Continuing Medical Education) and dues expense allowance, and retirement benefit contributions. The cost of physicians has risen above the amount of direct revenue-generating capacity of many physicians. This phenomenon has been driven by the integrated health systems in the community buying their "pipeline" of revenue, the primary care physician.

---

*This is an actual strategic plan. Information has been disguised to protect the confidentiality of the organization.

B. The new physician governance structure, although not mature, has greatly improved the physician environment. The new system consists of seven committees reporting to the Medical Executive Committee and the medical sections represented by a section chief on the Medical Executive Committee. This structure involves every member of the medical staff. This system has been in place for six months and physician opinion is very favorable thus far. Some refinement may be needed to more efficiently encompass some aspects of the clinic's operations.

C. The growth of the clinic is consuming capital in a decreasing reimbursement environment. The clinic has operated with a deficit since its inception six years ago. The continued growth of the clinic not only consumes growth capital but also increases the operating loss. This is caused by physician expense in a highly competitive environment. Decreasing reimbursement adds to the problem.

D. The payments for healthcare services are decreasing and demand is increasing. Government-funded healthcare is consistently decreasing reimbursement and the managed care is also decreasing or limiting increases in reimbursement.

E. HMO-type managed care is increasing, which increases the risk for the providers. This type of reimbursement pays for all care prospectively, placing the financial risk for providing care on the physician, medical group, hospital, and/or integrated healthcare system.

F. Managed care increases the opportunities for a group practice to acquire more patients. Employers and employees increasingly select managed care products to replace traditional forms of health insurance. Managed care in our environment is delivered by large organized groups, which causes a general shift from solo-practice physicians to group practices.

G. Managed care and decreasing profit margins require more sophisticated information systems and managers. Due to the risk involved in prepaid healthcare, providers must be well informed regarding income and consumption of resources. Managed care also demands sophisticated systems to control the utilization of resources and ensure that quality medical care is delivered.

H. Malpractice litigation is a growing concern. The medical-legal environment has increasing litigation and increasing financial judgments and settlements.

I. Service and product delivery expectations are changing. The nation's economy is increasingly a service-oriented economy with increasing expectations of more service. At the same time, the cost of healthcare has reached the point at which employers and government are not willing to pay for the level of medical care the population has become accustomed to.

J. The corporate culture of the integrated healthcare system, of which the clinic is a part, is changing. The system the clinic is a part of continues to grow into what will become a large, fully integrated healthcare delivery system, supplying healthcare to half the population of the eastern portion of the state.

K. The clinic currently has patient growth capacity. The clinic continues to grow as it positions itself to acquire more patients in the changing managed care environment. This excess capacity is expensive to acquire and maintain.

III. Strengths

A. High-quality, productive physicians. The clinic's minimum requirement for physicians is board certification. The interviewing process is stringent and normally weeds out individuals who will not function at the level expected by the physicians. This includes not only productivity but also patient, staff, and peer interpersonal relations.

B. High-quality, productive staff. The employees are selected using a multiple interview process in the attempt to identify the highest-quality candidates for each position. Training programs are used to increase the operational and customer service skills of the staff.

C. Managed care system human resource professionals available to support HR functions. Sophisticated human resource capability is available at a level that would not be possible in a clinic this size if it were not part of an integrated system.

D. New and state-of-the-art facilities and equipment. All facilities are three years old or less except the West Clinic. Equipment was purchased either new or like new. Availability of capital has allowed all facilities and equipment to be maintained in excellent condition.
E. State-of-the-art computer information systems. They replaced the clinic practice management and managed care computer and software system two years ago.
F. Strong financial backing. The clinic is a part of a managed care organization, an integrated healthcare delivery system with excellent financial performance and capital reserves. The system is investing in an expanded system to meet the needs of future reforms in the national system of healthcare delivery.
G. Capacity for growth, both physician and patient, in all clinic locations. The clinic is now positioned for additional patient capacity.
H. The clinic is a part of a large integrated healthcare system that is aggressively positioning itself for the future.

IV. Weaknesses

A. Some physicians less than highest quality. Some strategic decisions made in the past to maintain the primary care physician base of the system have resulted in the acquisition of less-than-desirable physicians.
B. Some physicians less productive than minimum standard. Discounting for excess physician supply, some physicians are not willing to produce at the minimum level of productivity established by the clinic.
C. Management staff experience limited to traditional patient care. Most of the management staff were promoted from within the clinic and lack depth of experience in other clinic environments. None of the management staff has experience in advanced managed care environments.
D. Physician compensation methodology not appropriate for the future. The current compensation plan is modeled around a fee-for-service reimbursement model. The future demands a managed care compensation model.

E. The central clinic not in an ideal location for growth. The central clinic is located in the older and poorer part of the metropolitan area. The largest complement of physicians is located in this clinic.
F. The central clinic medical record system's inefficiency. The centralized medical record storage and retrieval system in the central clinic drains human resources from patient care activities.
G. The clinic's negative net income. The financial drain on the system keeps the clinic very visible and a target for those critical of the expansion strategy and dollars being spent.

V. Assumptions

A. The clinic has little control over healthcare reform and it will have significant impact upon how we deliver medical care and how that care is paid for. Major healthcare reform at the national level will continue to be discussed and significant action will be taken at some point. Healthcare reform is already taking place in the Medicare program and at the state level, in particular with Medicaid. The public will continue to demand some form of healthcare reform to eliminate or decrease the uninsured population.
B. There will continue to be an increasing amount of regulatory agency, third-party intervention and/or consumer intervention. Agencies such as OSHA (Occupational Safety and Health Administration) and JCAHO (Joint Commission on Accreditation of Healthcare Organizations) will increase the amount of outside intervention on behalf of government and the consumer. A rational consolidation of overlapping oversight responsibilities is not forthcoming in the near future.
C. The risk-sharing form of managed care will continue gain market share in the local market. Managed care has increased from 5 percent to 20 percent of the market in a five-year period. At least one new managed care company is in town preparing to penetrate the market. Existing managed care companies are adding products and restructuring existing product to increase market share. Their goal is to gain new

business that currently does not have managed care as their medical coverage.

D. Revenue will continue to decrease but expenses will continue to increase at an equal or greater rate than inflation. The forces of healthcare reform will decrease reimbursement and/or the rate of increase in reimbursement. Healthcare technology will continue to advance, adding to the expense.

E. Malpractice and antitrust litigation will continue to increase and costs will increase. Our litigious society will increasingly sue until some form of tort reform is enacted. Tort reform may not make the cut in the healthcare reform arena. Antitrust litigation will increase for a period of time while the industry shakes out excessive capacity in some areas and limits managed care providers to the most cost-effective and highest quality. Risk management and litigation will become an increasing expense of the healthcare industry.

F. Right-sizing (matching staffing to service demand) of the clinic's operations will continue as well as right-sizing of the integrated system. This will increase management responsibilities. As the industry reengineers itself into a more efficient delivery system, fewer managers will be needed. This will increase the breadth of responsibilities for the remaining managers and radically change the style of management to a participatory form involving employees and physicians.

VI. Objectives, Goals, and Strategies

A. During year 2, decrease turnover by 20 percent.
   1. Use targeted selection process to hire staff. (April, year 2)
      a. All managers will attend targeted-selection classes.
      b. Targeted-selection process will be developed for all positions, detailing number of interviews and positions with responsibility for completing the interviews.
      c. Exit interviews will be completed.
   2. Consistently use the system's New Employee Orientation Program. (January, year 2)
      a. All new employees will attend the first scheduled orientation.

3. Enhance the clinic's orientation program and use consistently. (March, year 2)
   a. Monthly clinic orientations will be held.
   b. All new employees will attend the first scheduled orientation.
4. Increase in-service training.
   a. In-service objective developed. (See B.)

B. Increase the amount of in-service/CME offerings by 25 percent and increase attendance by 50 percent. (April, year 2)
1. Develop a clinic-wide in-service calendar.
   a. Management group will determine training needs on a quarterly basis.
   b. In-service calendar will be compiled quarterly.
2. Set a minimum standard number and type of in-services/CME hours managers must offer and employees must receive per year.
   a. Develop policy on CME qualification toward credit.
3. Make training a part of all staff's Evaluation and Development Plan on a yearly basis.

C. Attain a 99 percent patient satisfaction rate. (December, year 2)
1. All staff will attend the Quality Connection training course.
   a. Quality Connection course will be modified to increase emphasis on customer service and include CQI training.
2. Physicians will attend a physician customer service training course.
3. Physician Customer Service Committee will be developed.
4. Policies will be developed that empower the staff to immediately address customer services issues regardless of written policy.
   a. Quality Connection will emphasize these policies.
   b. Weekly staff meeting will emphasize these policies (part of standard agenda).

D. Decrease personnel expense by 5 percent relative to production in year 2.
1. Control overtime and agency utilization within budget.
   a. Review payroll and productivity reports with managers biweekly.

2. Increase utilization of part-time staff.
    a. Evaluate payroll and productivity reports for opportunities to improve efficiency.
3. Evaluate need for additional clerical staff to reduce nursing overtime.
    a. Evaluate payroll and productivity reports for opportunities to improve efficiency.
4. Increase the number of CQI teams evaluating the work processes to improve efficiency.
    a. Develop front office, business office, and nursing CQI teams in fourth quarter of year 1. Measurable results by end of first quarter of year 2.

E. Maintain FTEs (full-time equivalents) according to productivity in year 2.
1. Develop and distribute productivity reports to managers biweekly.
    a. Productivity reports developed and managers trained (January, year 2).
    b. Review payroll and productivity reports with managers biweekly.
2. Flex staffing with physician and patient load.
    a. Develop central physician schedule monitoring system.
    b. Coordinate staffing based on physician and patient schedule.

F. Develop new physician-compensation plan (July, year 2).
1. Use a physician-driven initiative through the Personnel and Compensation Committee.
    a. Develop productivity measure of an FTE physician.
    b. Develop base salary and bonus triggers that include productivity, customer satisfaction, outcomes, leadership, participation, etc.
2. Hire consulting firm to facilitate the initiative.
    a. The physicians need outside facilitation, since this initiative may result in decrease in income for some.

G. Enhance gross production in year 2 by 8 percent per patient, adjusted for increase productivity.
1. Using consulting firm, revise fee schedule using the RBRVS (Resource Based Relative Value System).

a. Use physician Finance and Operations Committee to develop new fee schedule.

2. Develop physicians'-coding workshop to improve the accuracy of CPT (Current Procedural Terminology) and ICD-9 (International Classification of Diseases) coding.
   a. Consulting firm to conduct initial physician training.
   b. Central business office will conduct ongoing training.
3. Audit for coding accuracy and feedback to physicians for continuous improvement.
   a. Finance and Operations Committee will develop a new fee ticket that addresses ICD-9 coding also.

H. Increase managed care profitability by 10 percent in year 2.
   1. Expand the utilization review team functions into ambulatory case management.
      a. Intake system will be refined to ensure capture of case management patients.
      b. PA (Physican's Assistant) will expand area of responsibility to include case management.
   2. Move all specialist providers to the standard contract rate (RBRVS).
      a. Aggressive contracting with nonstandard contract specialists to decrease nonstandard contracts by 50 percent.
   3. Develop specialty physician staff development plan (December, year 2).
      a. Start planning for decreasing the number of contracted specialty physicians.
      b. Evaluate the need for additional specialists in deficit areas.
   4. Gain access to surplus in Hospital Utilization Control Pools.
      a. Managed Care Committee to develop a recommendation to be acted upon by Medical Executive and Board of Directors.
      b. Managed Care Committee to develop distribution plan.

I. Develop new medical record system at headquarters (July, year 2).
   1. Medical record CQI team will address decentralization of

medical record department. Develop implementation plan by January, year 2.

2. Move medical records to areas of use on second and third floors.
    a. Medical records to be moved to second and third floors.
    b. First Data MR (Medical Records) ordering system to be modified.
3. Install and utilize pharmacy refill software and process.
    a. Software installed in satellite clinics (January, year 2).
    b. Central system and software after MR decentralization (July, year 2).

J. Expand patient base by 8 percent in year 2.
1. Utilize the system marketing department and local marketing firm to develop an awareness marketing plan for January, year 2 enrollment period.
2. Improve customer satisfaction.
    a. Goal C (attain a 99 percent patient satisfaction rate).
3. Recruit two to four internists or family practitioners to start by August, year 1.
    a. Utilize system medical staff development.
4. Develop new satellite location by August, year 2.
    a. Develop site selection criteria.
    b. Select site and build or finish out clinic space and bring into operation.
5. Expand existing site to new, larger site to facilitate growth.
    a. Develop site selection criteria.
    b. Select site and build or finish out clinic space and bring into operation.

K. Implement physician evaluation system (December, year 2).
1. Physician Professional Practices Committee to develop credentialing criteria for initial recruitment and retention.
2. After Goal F is completed, utilize measures developed as part of physician evaluation system to be developed by Professional Practices Committee.

L. Revise management and physician leadership reporting relationships (January, year 2).
1. Restructure management-reporting relationships to streamline and maximize management effectiveness.

a. Clearly delineate areas of responsibility using revised organizational chart.

2. Establish physician leadership-reporting relationships through committee structure.

a. Clearly delineate areas of responsibility using revised organizational chart.

M. Increase Ambuqual PQI score from 70 to 80 by the end of year 2.

1. Complete Ambuqual parameters that have not been addressed.

a. Appropriateness of service and patient risk minimization.

2. Start the Ambuqual cycle after completion of M.1.

a. Raise PQI targets from 70 to 80.

VII. Issues and Problems

A. Major.

1. Negative net income. The negative income attracts attention from those within the system who either don't agree with the system's development plans or don't understand the investments being made to execute that plan.

2. Physician leadership. The clinic lacks a full-time medical director. This significantly impacts the development and operation of the clinic in areas of physician involvement.

B. Minor.

1. MSO development. The development of a Medical Services Organization that utilizes clinic resources and expertise will decrease the amount of resources available for clinic development. This may cause physicians to feel something is being taken away from them in the form of management, power, and control.

2. Available management time. Management time is a limited resource and the dynamic development of the clinic and the MSO demands increasing amounts of time and expertise.

3. Inadequate management information. The clinic and system as a whole does not have adequate capability to turn the data we generate into usable management information.

VIII. Analysis

A. The clinic consumes capital for its operations and expansion. There is a limited source of capital and much demand on that source for strategic expansion.
B. The clinic lacks physician leadership supported by the physician group. This is crucial for any goal achievement that involves physicians or impacts physicians.
C. The development of the MSO will decrease the perceived power of the physician group.
D. Highly skilled management time is overloaded, compounded by the lack of physician leadership.
E. Inadequate management information is a result of limited management time.

IX. Alternative Solutions

A. Decrease rate of expansion and concentrate on adding patient volume and increasing efficiency.
   Pros: 1. Will conserve capital.
   2. Can improve overall efficiency due to overcapacity and inefficiency currently in system.
   Cons: 1. May lose a significant amount of needed market share in future if no capacity at a point in future.
   2. Any physician not hired today, will be hired by the competition.
   3. At some point in future, only the high-quality, productive physicians will be retained.
B. Hire full-time medical director.
   Pros: 1. This is a major deficit in the operation of the clinic.
   2. Physicians listen to physicians, not administrators.
   Cons: 1. Expense.
   2. If no physician acceptance of Medical Director, the results could be worse than not having one.
C. Involve the Medical Director and key staff in the development of the MSO.
   Pros: 1. MSO must have these people and skills to be successful.

2. This will expand the integrated system view into the clinic's operational plan.

Cons: 1. Individuals will feel threatened and insecure.

2. Physicians want to feel independent of other physician groups.

D. Increase management personnel and develop improved MIS (Management Information System).

Pros: 1. Adequate personnel and information to expand the clinic and manage in the most cost- effective manner.

Cons: 1. Expense.

X. Recommended Course of Action

A. Gain Board of Director's approval of this strategic plan.
B. Hire a full-time Medical Director.
C. Develop management information systems to support the strategic plan, using outside consultants and/or temporary help.
D. Evaluate the need for additional management staff after three to six months.

Managed Care Department of a Medical Clinic: Strategic Plan*

I. Purpose

The purpose of the Managed Care Department is to facilitate the delivery of quality, cost-effective medical care for members of the system's managed care programs. This service covers the metropolitan area and the central part of the state. We ensure access to highly trained medical providers, ensure accurate timely claims payment, and are dedicated to continuous improvement in customer service to our members.

II. Environmental analysis

A. Healthcare reform has been delayed until the next session of Congress. Employer groups are driving heath care reform by requiring that their healthcare provider deliver high-quality, cost-effective medical care for their employees.
B. Private practice physicians are unsure of any benefits associated with managed care, but many physicians are joining group practices to guarantee good incomes.
C. Hospitals are developing integrated healthcare systems, but not everyone involved understands managed care.
D. More services will be done on an outpatient basis, decreasing the utilization of patient bed days. Hospitals are developing ways to market their outpatient services to cover the loss of inpatient stays.

---

* This an actual strategic plan. Information has been disguised to protect the confidentiality of the organization.

III. Strengths and Weaknesses

A. Human

Strengths	The clinic has been involved with managed care contracts for the last six years. Infrastructures are in place to provide support for all managed care programs that the system will be providing.
Weaknesses	As membership grows, it will be difficult to hire experienced people from the community who understand managed care capitation, utilization, and contracting.

B. Facilities/Equipment

Strengths	Our new clinic and expansion of an existing clinic will increase access for more managed care patients. Integrating all physician groups affiliated with the system will ensure accessibility. Increased utilization of the communication network between satellites and contracted providers will shorten processing time of referrals for medically necessary care.
Weaknesses	Having quality providers to ensure access to all members. Integrating the hospital's managed care system with the clinic's system to reduce duplication of work.

C. Financial

Strengths	The system has funds to support a deficit in the managed care pools.
Weaknesses	Physicians who do not understand capitation and require more reimbursement for services when the fees paid to the clinic by the insurance company are preset. If one provider receives more than equitable reimbursement, the money has to come from another provider.

IV. Assumptions

A. Healthcare reform requirements will influence the direction of the department toward expansion.
B. Changes in capitation due to a very competitive marketplace.
C. Decrease in current membership if we do not provide services for all managed care companies in the area.
D. Sole-source providers receiving more reimbursement and no current strategy to contract with them.
E. Possible increase in membership without the providers in place to deliver the services.

V. Objectives, Goals, and Strategies

A. Establish budget guidelines that will result in budget neutrality by the end of year 1.
   1. Review current fee schedule for accurate fees.
   2. Audit past claims payment for accuracy; review past expenses before any changes are proposed.
   3. Access the environment for capitation of specialty services.
   4. Review current PCP (Primary Care Physician) capitation to ensure equal distribution of funds based on age/sex ratios.
B. Paperless referral system within five years.
   1. Request vendor information on available systems currently in place.
   2. Review current medical standards of care that would allow referrals to be handled more efficiently until electronic system in place.
   3. Work with HMOs to share cost of system when one is available.
   4. Work with PHO (Physician-Hospital Organizations) to integrate the referral process for all managed care patients.
C. Electronic claims processing within five years.
   1. Same strategy as referral system.
D. Physician-credentialing process streamlined for easy contracting process within one year.

1. Work with hospital-credentialing process to reduce duplication of work.
2. Utilize current quality assurance committee and managed care committee to review quality-of-care issues and utilization patterns, to maintain quality provider network.

E. Ambulatory case management program developed and implemented within one year.
   1. Develop data-base of current population.
   2. Review other systems currently in place. Adjust these systems to fit our organization.
   3. Make flowchart of proposed system and have physicians review for additional ideas.
   4. Start small; work with one group of the clinic's population and implement clinicwide participation as the process is redefined and streamlined.

VI. Issues and Problems

A. Major.
   1. Negative bottom line.
   2. MSO integration with current managed care department.

B. Minor.
   1. Limited growth in managed care plans.
   2. Recruiting of physicians.

VII. Analysis

A. Complete integration of managed care within the system. Many departments currently compete with one an other. This needs to be eliminated.

B. Changes within the capitation from the insurance company would change contracting strategies.

C. Pressure from physicians' group may delay the budget neutrality strategy.

D. Continue to involve physicians in management strategies of the managed care department.

E. Utilize training sessions available related to quality and case management to develop a highly skilled department.

VIII. Alternative Solutions

A. Move the managed care department to system headquarters.
   Pros: Shift the deficit from the clinic to the system.
   Cons: Support systems not in place for the system to administer the program. Decrease physician involvement.
B. Develop assistant manager for department and Medical Records to allow current manager more time to work with the system.
   Pros: More time devoted to area of clinic growth.
   Cons: Other responsibilities require supervision. The supervisor needs to be familiar with clinic and policies.

IX. Recommended Course of Action

Develop management team involving key members of Managed Care, PHO, and MSO. Make flowchart of the integration for the members of the team. Meet twice monthly to ensure that all members of the team have not lost sight of the vision of the department. Integrate the insurance companies into the process. Utilize the team to ensure a place in healthcare delivery for the system.

Operations Department of a Medical Clinic: Strategic Plan*

I. Purpose

The purpose of the Operations Department is to provide the clinic's staff with the direction, support, training, equipment, and facilities necessary to assist in the provision of high-quality medical care to our patients.

The Operations Department supports and is committed to the mission and values of the clinic.

II. Environmental Analysis

A. Patients are becoming informed consumers, shopping for the best care for their dollars.
B. Organizational right-sizing has placed increased demands on staff and managers.
C. Evaluation and streamlining of systems and processes is occurring at all levels of the clinic.
D. There is increased control of clinic operations by a variety of regulatory agencies: such as OSHA (Occupational Safety and Health Administration).
E. Third-party payers are more actively involved in assessing the quality of care being provided.
F. Demands for continuing education credits by many licensing and accrediting agencies are increasing.

*This is an actual strategic plan. Information has been disguised to protect the confidentiality of the organization.

III. Strengths

A. Staff willing to participate in CQI (Continuous Quality Improvement) process.
B. Computerized systems; PC network, billing system, etc.
C. Expert resources available; human resource, financial, etc.
D. High-quality, well-trained staff.
E. Large, flexible central clinic.

IV. Weaknesses

A. Expensive to convert nonpatient space to more productive space.
B. Physicians are often not supportive of staff or management.
C. Limited resources available to reward employees.
D. Lack of experienced managers and no trainers on staff.
E. Lack of fiscal responsibility by staff and physicians.

V. Assumptions

A. Healthcare reform will have definite impact on the way healthcare is delivered in the future.
B. There will be increasing demand placed on clinical staff as a result of regulation by federal agencies.
C. The Operations Department will be responsible for monitoring FTEs (Full-time Equivalents) and continued right-sizing of the clinic.
D. The money available for training, reward, and recognition of employees will be limited.

VI. Objectives and Strategies

A. Decrease turnover by 20 percent within one year.
   1. Develop a detailed orientation program.
   2. Implement a mentor program.
   3. Continue the multiple interview process.
   4. Establish an exit interview process.
B. Provide 12 hours in-service to each employee annually.
   1. Assign each manager a set number of in-services to provide.

2. Provide a calendar of pending in-services to employees.
3. Develop a core curriculum of classes offered on a routine basis.
4. Develop a database to store and track in-services attended by employees.

C. Double BIT/CQI teams within six months.
1. Keep BIT board current.
2. Post results of team results in newsletter.
3. Recruit team members.
4. Recognize team efforts.
5. Reward individual employees for significant contributions.

D. Attain 99 percent patient satisfaction rating within one year.
1. Increase customer service awareness through newsletter, section meetings, managers meetings', etc.
2. Restructure customer service training to emphasize quality care.
3. Benchmark the clinic against other organizations known for good customer service.

E. Maintain FTEs according to productivity and target control
1. Provide information bimonthly to managers (ie: FTEs/productivity).
2. Evaluate positions; restructure work processes.
3. Develop a method of flex staffing according to physician/patient load.

F. Decrease overtime to less than 2 percent annually.
1. Evaluate and revise processes to improve work flow.
2. Use part-time staff when possible.
3. Use flex staffing.

VII. Issues and Problems

A. Major.
1. Staff motivation and interest in training is affected by inappropriate physician behavior. The staff does not understand why they are held to a standard while the physicians often appear to incur no consequences for their behavior.
2. Availability of financial resources for training, reward, and recognition is restricted at times when the clinic is under

close scrutiny by our governing body. This causes frustration on the part of the staff and managers.

B. Minor.

1. Managers' time is often limited by the need to fill in for staff. This limits the time and energy available for managerial activity.
2. Managers are restricted by the lack of useful information. Because of time constraints, managers are not able to successfully interpret the raw data that is available. The ability to effectively manage manpower and resources is negatively impacted.

VIII. Analysis

The clinic's rapid growth has placed increased demand on an inexperienced management staff. The issues faced on a daily basis could more easily be dealt with by a more experienced management team. This inexperience has contributed to our high turnover rate, the difficulty of "living within our means," and a customer satisfaction rating that is less than acceptable by our own standard.

IX. Alternatives

A. Compensate for high turnover rate by hiring additional employees in a trainee position.

Pros:
1. Eliminates need for additional training/orientation dollars.
2. Ensures we have backups for staff when needed.

Cons:
1. Sends message to staff that we don't care if they stay with the clinic.
2. Adversely impacts FTEs.
3. Adversely impacts our customer service rating.

B. Increase management staff and add training staff.

Pros:
1. Ensures adequate staff for management of clinic and reduces stress on current managers.
2. Decreased workload on managers improves their morale and thereby improves staff morale.

Cons:
1. Expense.
2. Recruiting experienced staff.

C. Create a customer service department.
   Pros: 1. Improves our ability to make our customers happy immediately.
   2. Takes a large burden off our staff.
   Cons: 1. Expense.
   2. Sends message to staff that customer satisfaction is not their concern.
   3. Does not resolve customer service issues in the satellites.

X. Recommended Course of Action

A. Gain Executive Director's approval of plan.
B. Evaluate the need for additional staff and managers on a case-by-case basis.
C. Develop the systems necessary to provide adequate information for the managers.
D. Provide additional training for inexperienced managers.

Regional Medical Center: Strategic Plan*

INTRODUCTION

Regional Medical Center (RMC) is a not-for-profit healthcare facility, licensed to conduct business in the State. Management and trustees, in recognizing the practice of medicine, medical technology, utilization of hospital services, and society are undergoing a fundamental change, have been concerned about the future direction and role of the hospital within the community it serves. In response and in order to ensure the future growth and prosperity of the hospital, the Governing Board has developed a strategic plan for the organization.

The purpose of this effort is to enable the hospital to evaluate present programs while looking ahead and to establish the climate and direction of the institution to move forward in the dynamic healthcare environment.

MISSION, VALUES, AND GOALS

Our Mission

Regional Medical Center is a private, not-for-profit entity incorporated under the laws of the State. Its primary mission is to provide a system for the delivery of quality patient-centered healthcare services that benefit individuals, families, and the communities of this region of the state. The organization will strive to be the provider of choice for hospital and healthcare services in its service area and to be perceived as a responsive, innovative provider of selected services.

---

*This is an actual strategic plan. Information has been disguised to protect the confidentiality of the organization.

Our Values

We believe that the guiding and motivating values that have led us, and will be even more important as we continue to move forward, include the following:

COMPASSION
We believe that each person–patient, family member, or caregiver–is unique in health, in sickness, in life, and in death. Each is to receive our respect, our care, our concern, our appreciation . . . our empathy.

COMMUNITY
We value its well-being and are committed to its progress. In addition to our services, we provide an important corporate contribution, expressed through involvement with the people and organizations that vitalize, energize, and support our region.

TEAMWORK
Our success stems from teamwork. We recognize the equal value and individual contribution of each member of our team. We believe in mutual regard for each other and for our patients. We encourage teamwork by working together respectfully, communicating openly, and supporting the expression of differing opinions and perspectives.

SERVICE EXCELLENCE
Our excellence is born of individual commitment to the highest personal potential. We realize that if all reach our individual potentials we can achieve service to others that can be the source of our growth and well-being, while maintaining a financially successful organization.

PROGRESS AND INNOVATION
We understand the need for these attributes in patient care and organizational management. While pursuing the tradition and wisdom of those who have gone before us, we seek new information and state-of-the-art technology. We welcome new insights, new techniques, new ideas . . . and will remain leaders in the healthcare of our community.

Our Goals

To support our mission, we adopt the following organizational goals.

1. *Growth:* To increase and expand our presence in the service area through repackaging existing services and adding new services based upon market needs and desires.
2. *Finance:* To maintain an annual return on investments equal to or above the regional norm for meeting the full financial requirements of the organization and to maintain competitive prices.
3. *Customer:* To continually develop policies that promote participation, communication, and cooperation among members of the Board, management, medical staff, community, and the various groups that reside in the service area.
4. *Human Resources:* To provide competitive wages, a quality work environment, and employment stability through internal and external development and incentive programs.
5. *Service:* To continually promote the mutual advantages of cooperation and quality service delivery among the hospital, its employees, the medical staff, and its communities in providing healthcare services.

SITUATION ANALYSIS

Industry Trends

The healthcare industry is currently in the middle of a fundamental change that began in the 1960s and 1970s and is expected to continue but will culminate in the 1990s with the development of a new healthcare corporation. Environmental trends that have placed significant stress on the healthcare system and have stimulated the changes can be categorized into societal and healthcare basic trends. Societal trends are:

Stabilizing economy
Demographic shifts
Moving to wellness lifestyle
Technology push

Healthcare basic trends are:

Continued pressure to moderate costs
Access to capital
Utilization slide
Alternative delivery explosion
Ethical balance

The U.S. has emerged from its deepest postwar recession into a period of relative stability. Long-term forecasts predict mild growth rates and moderate inflation rates. A major concern will continue to be the federal deficit. Major demographic shifts, such as the maturing of the population, higher educational levels, dual-income families, as well as single heads of households, are resulting in new demands for healthcare. People are demanding more information about their health and are using that information to make change. Technological changes have stimulated increased competition due to greater availability of low-cost, reliable, maintenance-free products. Thus, an informed public is desiring personal, convenient care in new treatment settings, as a result of having an active lifestyle and being extremely pushed for time.

There will be continued pressure on reducing costs through reimbursement freezes and discounts. Capital will be available though harder to access. Utilization patterns will continue to shift to lower-cost/less intensive treatment patterns, but will still be moderated by an increasing elderly population. Alternative delivery systems (PPOs, HMOs) are also anticipated to expand, but at a slower rate than seen in the past. With changes in technology, reimbursement systems, and new treatment patterns, ethical issues not previously addressed will need to be addressed and resolved.

Major medical trends based on societal pressures as well as technology are:

- Continued slide in utilization as more services move to the outpatient setting
- Inpatients will be more acutely ill and thus require greater use of intensive care units
- Increased use of multidisciplinary teams in patient care
- Greater use of technology that will decrease the length of stay
- Increase in noninvasive surgical procedures

- Improvements in prevention, diagnosis, and treatment through early detection programs
- Consolidation of services around technology
- Increased use of automation and computers
- Streamlined services through increased coordination
- More emphasis on regionalized treatment with follow-up services in the outpatient and home settings
- Diffusion of MRI (magnetic resonance imaging) technology is anticipated to follow the diffusion of CT (computerized tomography) scanners

Other major trends affecting the healthcare system:

- Healthcare providers are at greater financial risk
- Restructuring of the U.S. health insurance industry
- As major buyers, employers are taking action

From the above brief analysis of trends in the healthcare industry, it can be seen that there are many challenges and opportunities facing the healthcare system in general as well as locally. Strategic imperatives for the management of the new healthcare corporation are:

- Managing risks
- Managing costs
- Managing ethical and legal issues
- Information systems for decision making
- New performance incentives
- Integrating new forms of capital
- New governance
- New partnerships

RMC SWOT Analysis

STRENGTHS of Regional Medical Center

Financial Status

Location

Dedicated Caring Staff

Quality of nursing care
Strong medical staff

Supportive employee group
Experienced, loyal, long-term staff

Community Support

Supportive people in city
Demographics–young population
Local industry support

Progressive Programs/Services

Wellness program
Educational programs
Women's Center–gives RMC a head start
Outpatient services

Leadership

Strong administration, when given opportunity
Medical staff access to administration

Hospital Image

Good reputation
No "tie-ins"
Only area community-owned hospital

Physical Plant

WEAKNESSES of Regional Medical Center

Staff Awareness and Involvement

Lack of esprit de corps
Weak/improper personnel in certain areas
Lack of constructive problem solving from physicians
Perceived lack of communication system
Understanding of marketing/advertising/PR

Board

Structure
Poorly educated Board
Understanding of its role

Response Behavior

React more than act
Direction is hazy
Unclear mission statement (slogan)
Slowness to respond
Follower, not a leader

Nursing Problems

Nursing shortage and retention
Nursing support services
Lack of aides, permanent positions

Organizational Relationships

Board/medical staff relations
Community perception, hospital/medical staff relations

Tools to Build Direction

Lack of subspecialties, e.g., neurosurgery, orthopedics
Lack of expertise, market niche
Lack of medical office complex on RMC property

Patient Service Problems

Lack of patient representative
Hotel services, e.g., food, cleanliness

Service Quality Problems

Admission procedure, lack of privacy
ER problems
Physical therapy
No incentive for guest relations

Physical Plant Problems

ER
ICU
CCU (cardiac care unit)

Fund Development

OPPORTUNITIES for Regional Medical Center

Employee Development

Recapture employee morale
Capitalize on employee strengths
Promote "we care" policy
Admissions staff, work with physicians

Development and Support of Key Publics

Bonding with key physicians
Enhance physicians' practice through marketing
Solidify Board/medical staff relationship

New Programs

Diabetes care
Reestablish cardiac rehabilitation
Lung/respiratory care center
Ophthalmology center
Hospice/home center
Oncology program
Health club

Attractive Market Options

Exploit convenience
Target 30-50 age groups and high-income group
Target the undecided
Build on community hospital concept

Corporate Outreach

Diversify and network
Prepare for alternative delivery system (ADS)
Dialogue with industry
Construct medical office building, including support

Develop and Improve ER

THREATS Facing Regional Medical Center

Competition

More competition between hospital and clinics
Other hospital-aggressive physician recruiting
Loss of nursing staff
Increased marketing by regional delivery organization
Physicians/hospitals duplicating services
Service duplication erodes financial base

Current Relationships

Status quo, no change
Board/medical staff problems grow
Improper reaction/action to threats
Continued conflicts–Board, medical staff, administration
Board ignorance of modern hospital concept

Limitations to Growth

Lack of subspecialty support
Physician support of hospital recruitment effort
Nursing complexities, adjustment to delivery of care

Reimbursement

Changing reimbursement
Alternative delivery system (ADS) imposed on community
Declining inpatient census

Local Economy

RMC STRATEGIC ISSUES

As the future is considered, the current situation as well as industry trends have to be considered so the organization can position itself to be able to respond in an effective and efficient manner. Challenges facing management are:

- Solving difficult problems caused by widespread changes;
- Managing for short- and long-term well-being;
- Engaging the total organization and its staff to produce their best.

Based upon the strengths, weaknesses, opportunities, and threats facing the organization, the strategic issues facing Regional Medical Center are: to enhance Board, medical staff, and administration relationships; to establish a defined direction; and to improve processes to provide quality patient care.

Organizational Issues

With the increase in competition for the healthcare dollar, it is necessary for the above parties to be able to work together for the effective and efficient operation of the corporation. To develop this relationship each party need to be examined and hard decisions need to be made to facilitate the future growth and development of Regional Medical Center. Basic questions that need to be answered with decisions made to smooth interrelationships are:

Board:

1. How should it be organized to do business in an effective manner?
2. What processes should be used to make effective and efficient decisions?
3. What is the appropriate role?

Medical Staff:
1. How should leadership be chosen?
2. Should incentives be in place for leadership?
3. If so, what should they be?
4. How can it support development of the "medical center"?

Administration:
1. What should the structure be to do business in an efficient manner?
2. What mechanisms are needed to assure that management is allowed to do what it is hired to do?

As an organization evolves, it is necessary to continually appraise structure and relationships to assure a viable organization. An important part of this process, particularly as the environment changes and with greater proportions of revenue coming from nontraditional (noninpatient) sources, is assessing how much risk the organization is willing to incur as this will, in part, determine program development options.

Program Development Issues

With all the changes that are occurring in the healthcare field, it is necessary to concentrate efforts in a few select areas and then use a variety of techniques to defend your chosen areas. This strategy will allow Regional Medical Center to build on a "community 'we care' concept" while also being able to develop as a "medical center."

Areas of perceived strength or opportunity upon which to build are:

Strength	*Opportunity*
Wellness Program	Diabetes Care
Women's Center	Cardiac Rehabilitation
Outpatient Services	Lung/Respiratory Care
Education Programs	Ophthalmology
Surgery: General	Hospice/Home Care
Ambulatory	Oncology
Ophthalmology	Health Club
Chemical Dependency Unit	
Emergency Room	
Pulmonary Diseases	
Gastroenterology	

To determine potential target areas for program development, basic questions that need to be addressed are:

1. Who is the current leader?
2. What is the strength of the leader?
3. What is the leader's weakness?
4. What is our strength?
5. What is our weakness?
6. How can programmatic areas be combined to give a distinct advantage to RMC?
7. Will the medical staff provide support?

The aim of this process should be to develop "top of the mind" awareness for Regional Medical Center in a few selected areas. This approach should help in building a "medical center" image while capitalizing on the "community" concept. In general, all services should benefit as the same "quality" factors would be instituted across the total organization.

Service Quality Issues

As the healthcare system and organization evolve, careful consideration needs to be given to current procedures and processes related to the provision of services as well as the communication systems. The various publics, i.e., Board, physicians, employees, customers, need to know either implicitly or explicitly the direction of the organization if they are to help in moving the organization forward.

Basic areas to consider in addressing this issue are:

1. How do we communicate with our publics? Is it effective?
2. How do we listen to our customers (publics)?
3. How do we handle complaints?
4. How can we tap the creativity of our staff?
5. What new methods/techniques for the provision of services are needed?

The result of this process should be to examine current methods of communication with and obtaining input from various groups. This effort should build team spirit and improve morale as well as build processes to provide opportunities for job enrichment. All aspects of this effort should lead to enhancing the "caring attitude" across the total organization and consequently create a distinct advantage for Regional Medical Center.

OBJECTIVES AND ACTION PLANS

A. *Growth Objective*: To increase the service area market share by at least 3 percent by FY5 through repackaging existing services and the addition of new services based upon the market needs and desires.

To accomplish this objective RMC will maintain its role as a full-service community-based healthcare organization while targeting specific program areas for growth and development. Program areas selected for emphasis are based on research findings as areas upon which RMC already has significant name recognition or areas that currently do not have a comprehensive program. Program areas selected will directly and/or indirectly impact all services through service improvements, utilization, staffing, etc.

Actions Required to Accomplish the Objective	Required Resources
1. Expand Women's Center	
a. Continue to reevaluate program offerings and package based on target market.	Patient Input Market Research
b. Continue to appraise the program with the intent of finding ways to improve the service. 1. What else is needed? 2. New ways to package 3. Consistent logo/theme	Patient Input Market Research
c. Be prepared to respond quickly to competitors' moves.	Market Surveillance
2. Develop Comprehensive Oncology Program	
a. Determine range of services provided by other area providers.	Market Surveillance
b. Determine range of services provided by cancer centers across the country.	Program Research
c. Develop a list of services available through cancer centers along with resources required.	Management Time

d. Determine strengths and weaknesses of current providers.	Market Surveillance Market Research Document
e. Determine additional programs to offer at RMC based on service area voids plus weaknesses in current programs.	Management Time
f. Determine additional physicians that are needed to support growth of the program.	Management Time
3. Expand Wellness Program	
a. Visit other programs.	Management Time
b. Determine range of options to offer through program along with resources required.	Management Time Program Research
c. Determine desired range of services to be provided, if resources were not a problem. 1. Increase efforts in prevention 2. Increase efforts in rehabilitation 3. How to expand to industry? 4. How to offer to community?	Management Time
d. Determine options to phase in desired range of services along with resource requirements.	Management Time
e. Provide appropriate facility for current and future program offerings.	Architect Facility Cost: Undetermined to date
4. Explore relationships with healthcare providers in outlying communities that will facilitate referral relationships.	Management Time Medical Staff Time
5. Enhance Medical Staff Capabilities and Composition	
a. Develop a physician tracking system to actively monitor at a minimum. 1. Number of admits by physician 2. Number of admits by specialty 3. Age of individual physicians 4. Average age by specialty 5. Mix of primary care physicians vs. specialty physicians	Management Time Medical Staff Time

b. Have at least two physicians actively practicing at RMC for each major service and/or product line. — Management Time; Medical Staff Time

c. Active physicians in any one specialty area should provide a variety of practice options.

d. Develop mechanisms to align physicians with RMC. — Management Time; Medical Staff Time

1. Ensure appropriate office space is available.
2. Target number of physicians to be contacted each month to determine their needs.
3. Actively solicit their input.

e. Make a commitment to actively maintain the desired medical staff complement. — Board Time; Medical Staff Time

f. Ensure that numbers and types of physicians needed to support programs of emphasis are *actively* practicing at RMC, specifically:

Specialty	Needed Total of Actively Practicing Physicians	Additional Needed	Time Frame	Justification
OB/GYN	8	3	FY3	Program Development Increase Market Share
Pediatrics	7	2	FY3	Complement OB/GYN Anticipate Retirement
Hematology/Oncology	3	1 1	FY1 FY2	Program Development Increase Market Share Expand Market Area
Radiation Therapy	2 to 3	1	FY2	Program Development

g. Ensure that numbers and types of physicians needed to complement current staff and improve access to medical care are *actively* practicing at RMC, specifically:

Specialty	Needed Total of Actively Practicing Physicians	Additional Needed	Time Frame	Justification
General Surgery	6	1 1	FY3 FY5	Increase Market Share Anticipate Retirement

Orthopedics	5	2	FY1	Increase Market Share
Pulmonary Medicine	2	1	FY1	Increase Market Share
Chemical non-invasive	3	1	FY1	Increase Market Share
Cardiology Dependency	2	1	FY1	Increase Market Share
Neurology	2	1 1	FY1 FY3	Increase Market Share Complement Orthopedics
Neuro-surgery	1	1	FY1	Increase Market Share Complement Orthopedics
Nephrology	2	1	FY1	Increase Market Share

B. *Finance Objective*: To maintain an annual return on gross patient revenues of at least 10 percent and/or an operating margin of at least 6 percent for meeting the full financial requirements of the organization while maintaining competitive prices.

Due to the dynamics of the healthcare system and to ensure access to financial markets, the financial status of RMC needs to be closely monitored to ensure a viable organization in the short as well as the long term. In addition, costs also have to be monitored so that products that are developed and promoted are beneficial to the organization.

Actions Required to Accomplish the Objective	Required Resources
1. Monitor the following key financial ratios on a monthly basis and take appropriate action as needed. a. Days in A/R b. Average Payment Period c. Deductible Percentages d. Mark Up	Financial Management Time Administration Time Board Time
2. Monitor all the financial ratios as found in the financial analysis section of the complete document on an annual basis.	Financial Management Time Administration Time Board Time

3. Develop the ability to determine the cost of services by December FY1.	Financial Management Time Administration Time Consultant
4. Implement cost-saving activities, where possible.	Management Time
5. Explore opportunities to expand the financial base in related and/or unrelated activities that will benefit the organization.	Financial Management Time Administration Time

C. *Customer Objective*: To continually develop operational policies that promote participation, communication, and cooperation among members of the Board, management, medical staff, community, and the various groups that are found in the service area.

To accomplish this objective, concerted action is needed in two areas (Board role clarification and market monitoring), which should facilitate the hospital's becoming a more competitive and aggressive organization in the region's healthcare system. The actions are based on streamlining the decision-making process and bringing objectivity and conformity to monitoring processes.

Actions Required to Accomplish the Objective	Required Resources
1. Determine the role of the Board by June FY1 so as to align itself with the current healthcare industry climate considering the specific implications to RMC. a. Functions and responsibilities should be defined. b. Board composition should be studied and recommendations implemented.	Board Time Consultant Legal Assistance
2. Board educational sessions should be conducted on a semiannual basis on pertinent topics as expressed by the Board.	Board Time Administration Time Outside Parties
3. Develop objective and consistent mechanisms to listen to the marketplace to facilitate program development and monitor change.	Marketing Management Time Consultant

a. Track patient attitudes and perceptions in a consistent and objective fashion.
b. Target specific programs/groups to research to facilitate program development.
c. Conduct general research every 18 to 24 months.
d. All monitoring mechanisms should be administered by the same department with results going to appropriate parties.

D. *Human Resources Objective:* To continually provide competitive wages, provide a quality working environment, and ensure employment stability through internal and external development and incentive programs.

A valuable resource to every organization is its employees. Therefore, a variety of methods needs to be evaluated and implemented to facilitate the attraction and retention of employees. At the same time, methods have to be instilled to ensure that employee skills are used to their fullest potential and the organization's benefit.

Actions Required to Accomplish the Objective	Required Resources
1. Implement mechanisms to ensure a service management philosophy throughout the organization with appropriate rewards.	H.R. Management Time Marketing Management Time Nursing Management Time
2. Promote the use of internal "teams" to generate ideas within the organization to assist in solving problems.	H.R. Management Time Marketing Management Time Administration Time

a. Criteria for involvement
b. Method of selection
c. Duration of "team"
d. Necessary time
e. Method of recognition

E. *Service Objective:* To continually promote mutual advantages between the hospital and the medical staff in providing healthcare services.

When all the changes in the healthcare environment are considered, greater risks are being placed on the providing entities. Therefore, it is becoming more important than seen in the past to develop program opportunities in new ways to the benefit of multiple providers. Consequently, programs should be developed in such a manner as to be advantageous to parties involved either directly or indirectly.

Actions Required to Accomplish the Objective	Required Resources
1. Develop programs that allow equity ownership or joint ownership with physicians on the active staff at the hospital.	Administration Time Medical Staff Time
2. Develop mechanisms that allow for closer affiliation between the medical staff and hospital. a. Computer link to hospital b. Group purchasing c. Customer relations d. Medical office building e. Physician amenities, e.g., dining room, lounge	Management Time Medical Staff Time
3. Develop internal mechanisms to evaluate and streamline operations and costs for the hospital as well as an office practice. a. Office Management b. Management Engineering Program	Finance Management Time Consultant/Program

	Actions	Impact Corporate Objectives	Responsible Party	FY1				FY2				FY3				FY4			
				1	2	3	4	1	2	3	4	1	2	3	4	1	2	3	4
A1.	Women's Center	Growth	Administration																
	a. Market Research	Finance	Marketing Dept.																
	b. Program Appraisal	Service	Finance																
	c. Market Surveillance	Customer	Product Mgr.																
A2.	Oncology Program	Growth	Administration																
	a. Program Research	Finance	Marketing Dept.																
	b. Market Research/ Surveillance	Service Customer	Finance Product Mgr.																
A3.	Wellness Program	Growth	Administration																
	a. Program Research	Customer	Marketing Dept.																
	b. Determine Programs	Service	Finance																
	c. Provide Facility		Product Mgr.																
A4.	Medical Staff Composition	Growth Finance	Board Administration																
	a. Tracking System	Service	Medical Staff																
	b. Physician Bonding	Customer																	
B1.	Financial Ratio	Finance	Finance																
B2.	Analysis	Growth	Administration																
	a. Qtrly. Monitoring	Service																	
	b. Annual Monitoring																		
B3.	Determine Costs	Finance Growth Service	Finance Administration Consultant																
B4.	Financial Development	Finance Growth Customer	Finance Administration																

	Actions	Impact Corporate Objectives	Responsible Party	FY1 1	FY1 2	FY1 3	FY1 4	FY2 1	FY2 2	FY2 3	FY2 4	FY3 1	FY3 2	FY3 3	FY3 4	FY4 1	FY4 2	FY4 3	FY4 4
C1.	Board Role	Customer Growth Finance	Board Consultant Service																
C2.	Market Monitoring a. Patient Attitudes b. Program Perf. c. General Market	Customer Growth Finance Service	Marketing Consultant Administration																
D1.	Service Management	Human Res. Growth Customer	Human Res. Marketing Nursing																
D2.	Internal Problem Solving	Human Res. Growth Customer Service	Human Res. Marketing Administration																
E1.	Equity Ownership	Service Customer Growth Finance	Management Medical Staff																
E2.	Closer Affiliation Physician/Hospital	Service Customer Growth Finance	Management Medical Staff																
E3.	Mechanisms to Streamline Oper.	Service Customer Growth	Management Medical Staff Consultant																

Metropolitan Medical Center: Strategic Plan*

INTRODUCTION

Metropolitan Medical Center's vision is to be a regional provider of healthcare services. Strategic activities focus on expanding relationships with others and on service delivery aspects to foster a stronger partnership between the Medical Center, its medical staff, and the communities served.

The ultimate goal of any strategy set forth in this document is to deliver quality services and programs that meet the needs of the market and are competitive with other providers' service offerings. In addition, the plan is geared toward maintaining the public's perception of the Medical Center and its staff as leaders in healthcare.

In order to fulfill our mission, MMC will develop comprehensive, community-oriented, patient-centered services and referral-oriented programs in a select number of areas. Strategic activities will be dedicated to the delivery of quality, competitive, market- and customer-oriented services and programs. These efforts will ensure that the hospital and its staff are area healthcare leaders and that the financial strength/viability of all involved will be strengthened.

MMC will implement three primary strategies as vehicles for guiding future decision making and achieving its goals: (1) Affiliation Program Development; (2) Service Delivery; and (3) Physician Support.

---

*This is an actual strategic plan. Information has been disguised to protect the confidentiality of the organization.

Strategy: Affiliation Program Development

Program Title: Affiliation with Healthcare Organizations

Program Objective: To simultaneously confirm a strategy and business plan for affiliations with healthcare organizations and to secure one or two additional relationships with outlying facilities by year end FY5.

Actions:	Target Completion Date:
1. Establish/reaffirm goals of MMC in securing linkages with area hospitals.	1st quarter, FY5
2. Identify programs/services available from MMC to affiliate hospitals. • assess MMC resource availability	1st quarter, FY5
3. Examine fit of existing corporate structure vis-á-vis outreach efforts.	1st quarter, FY5
4. List area healthcare organizations that may benefit from affiliation with MMC. • identify characteristics of these facilities ✓ financial status ✓ bed size ✓ distance from city ✓ medical staff	1st quarter, FY5
5. Conduct research to discover potential affiliate hospital needs. • questionnaire • follow-up visits	1st quarter, FY5
6. Develop business plan and budget.	2nd quarter, FY5
7. Corporate restructuring, if necessary.	2nd quarter, FY5

Resources Required:	Estimated Capital Costs:
Human	Legal fees Research/consulting: $25,000

Total Estimated Capital Costs: $25,000

Responsible Department: Administration

Status Report:

Strategy: Affiliation Program Development

Program Title: Affiliation with Industry

Program Objective: To develop a business plan during FY5 for establishing affiliation agreements with area employers that focus on the delivery of preventive healthcare services and programs.

Actions:	**Target Completion Date:**
1. Survey industries to determine interest in healthcare activities/services and other healthcare concerns. • conduct area employer survey or make personal calls to area employers to begin building relationships	2nd quarter, FY5
2. List activities/services that MMC can offer to area industry. • evaluate resource requirements, in particular human resources	2nd quarter, FY5
3. Based on the survey results, list activities/services that MMC does not currently provide for which there is interest. • identify development programs stating priority	3rd quarter, FY5
4. Form hospital committee of clinical and administrative staff. • develop business plan and budget for service delivery • create marketing plan • identify personnel needs • select project manager	4th quarter, FY5

Resources Required:
Human

Estimated Capital Costs:
Research/Consulting: $26,000

Total Estimated Capital Costs: $26,000

Responsible Department: Administration

Status Report:

Strategy: Affiliation Program Development

Program Title: Affiliation with Universities

Program Objective: To explore and prioritize activities for developing relationships in clinical areas with area universities and other technical training/educational institutions by June FY5.

Actions:	**Target Completion Date:**
1. List potential partners for educational programs. • local universities • nearby medical school	1st quarter, FY5
2. Formulate task force of MMC staff and university staff to identify program components and develop arrangements for cooperation.	1st quarter, FY5
3. Identify educational needs of MMC staff (hospitals and physicians).	2nd quarter, FY5
4. Identify educational/service needs of the community which MMC is currently unable to provide, e.g., industrial hygiene.	2nd quarter, FY5
5. Prioritize activities to be implemented.	3rd quarter, FY5

Resources Required:	**Estimated Capital Costs:**
Human	
Capital Equipment	
Facilities	

Total Estimated Capital Costs:

Responsible Department: Administration

Status Report:

Strategy: Service Delivery

Program Title: Outpatient Service Delivery

Program Objective: To have a strategy and site plan for outpatient service delivery by year-end FY5.

Actions:	**Target Completion Date:**
1. Establish physician/board/administration/ hospital staff task force to study outpatient service delivery and develop recommendations on action(s).	1st quarter, FY5
2. Examine various services regularly accessed for outpatient services, i.e., ancillaries, that might be integrated into an outpatient service department. • other services project to move to outpatient setting • explore potential for preferred arrangements for overnight accommodations and transportation for families of patients coming from out of town.	1st quarter, FY5
3. Develop 5-year volume projections by department/function for outpatient services.	1st quarter, FY5
4. Evaluate service delivery alternatives, be sure to include customer (physician and patient) expectations. • Information needs • Tracking systems	2nd quarter, FY5
5. Determine functional space requirements. • review master site plan	2nd quarter, FY5
6. Agree on strategy for outpatient service delivery. • develop business plan that reflects strategy	3rd quarter, FY5

Resources Required:
Human
Facilities

Estimated Capital Costs:
Consulting: $30,000
Potential renovation/new

Total Estimated Capital Costs: $30,000

Responsible Department: Administration

Status Report:

Strategy: Service Delivery

Program Title: Chest Pain ER

Program Objective: To have implemented a coordinated Chest Pain ER by year end FY5.

Actions:	**Target Completion Date:**
1. Document ER utilization for chest pain or cadiac-related reasons. • time of day • day of week • length of stay • disposition of patient • staffing • physician; coverage/cardiac capabilities • evaluate functional feasibility of another "track" • work with cardiologist/nursing/support staff on ways to enhance care provided and develop recommendations	1st quarter, FY5
2. Develop marketing plan for Chest Pain ER.	1st quarter, FY5
3. Communicate plan internally to hospital and medical staff.	1st quarter, FY5
4. Implement marketing plan.	1st quarter, FY5

Resources Required:
Human

Estimated Capital Costs:
Marketing material: $5,000

Total Estimated Capital Costs:

Responsible Department: Nursing administration

Status Report:

Strategy: Service Delivery

Program Title: Cancer Treatment Program

Program Objective: To have in place by June FY5 a strategy for the development of a coordinated cancer treatment program.

Actions:	**Target Completion Date:**
1. Study needs of current cancer patients regarding: • services used at MMC • services used that MMC does not provide • changing treatment patterns • reimbursement trends	1st quarter, FY5
2. Investigate requirements for a Certified Comprehensive Cancer Program.	1st quarter, FY5
3. Evaluate need/calculate demand, reimbursement for services not currently provided.	2nd quarter, FY5
4. Study existing services in the community, with attention given to home health and hospice.	2nd quarter, FY5
5. Clarify and document strategy for the delivery of cancer treatment services.	3rd quarter, FY5

Resources Required:	**Estimated Capital Costs:**
Human	$15,000
Total Estimated Capital Costs:	$15,000
Responsible Department:	Administration and Nursing Administration

Status Report:

Strategy: Service Delivery

Program Title: Senior Services

Program Objective: To investigate the need and demand for senior care services by July FY6.

Actions:	**Target Completion Date:**
1. Conduct focus groups of 65+ population (or appropriate age) to gather information on needs/demands.	1st quarter, FY6
2. Examine use of existing services such as Wellness Center for specific and special programs for this population.	1st quarter, FY6
3. Analyze 65+ population demographics and health service consumption. • identify demand for service over 5-year period	1st quarter, FY6
4. Study existing services available and accessible to elderly at hospitals and in community.	2nd quarter, FY6
5. Clarify and document strategy for gerontology services. • define services to be provided • locate/identify resource needs ✓ physical plant ✓ medical staff • explore linkages with others for delivery of certain components of service ✓ nursing home ✓ education ✓ service organizations • perform feasibility	3rd quarter, FY6

Resources Required:
Human

Estimated Capital Costs:
$10,000

Total Estimated Capital Costs:

Responsible Department: Marketing

Status Report:

Strategy: Service Delivery

Program Title: Women's Center Development

Program Objective: To conduct a study by year-end FY3 to further define the hospital's role in delivery of Women's services.

Actions:	**Target Completion Date:**
1. Establish physician/administration/ hospital staff task force to study issues and develop recommendations for action.	1st quarter, FY3
2. Examine current facility to identify strengths and weaknesses. • determine when current renovations will be complete	1st quarter, FY3
3. Study other area women's centers to understand competition's capabilities.	2nd quarter, FY3
4. Perform feasibility study to include: • identification of demand for service • survey of medical staff • focus groups of consumers and physicians • facility needs • cost/benefit	3rd quarter, FY3
5. Select project manager, if appropriate.	4th quarter, FY3

Resources Required:	**Estimated Capital Costs:**
Human	$10,000
Total Estimated Capital Costs:	$10,000
Responsible Department:	Nursing Administration, Obstetricians, and Marketing

Status Report:

Strategy: Physician Support

Program Title: Physician Resources Planning

Program Objective: To develop a mutually beneficial strategy and plan for medical staff development and support by July FY5

Actions:	Target Completion Date:
1. Establish a minimum number of physicians to contact per month to determine their concerns, needs.	1st quarter, FY5
2. Establish medical staff development task force to study issues and develop coordinated recommendations. • mix and depth of clinical coverage • number and support needed for priority program areas • interest in office enhancement services • effective communication systems ✓ inform of new services/programs/ staff ✓ results reporting	1st quarter, FY5
3. Develop medical resources development plan that addresses: • recruitment needs • development of supporting services • existing physician needs	3rd quarter, FY5

Resources Required:	Estimated Capital Costs:
Human	Consulting: $15,000
Capital Equipment	Variable by outcome

Total Estimated Capital Costs:

Responsible Department: Administration

Status Report:

Strategy: Physician Support

Program Title: Multi-purpose Building

Program Objective: To determine the need for a building that provides support services to the medical staff, the community, and the hospital by year end FY6.

Actions:	**Target Completion Date:**
1. Assess need for additional practices. • new practice(s) • satellite; full time, time share • support requirements	1st quarter, FY6
2. Include plans for related services. • ancillaries • hotel • senior services • educational outlet • retail space • healthcare societies, e.g., American Heart Association, American Lung Association, etc.	1st quarter, FY6
3. Evaluate existing/vacant available space. • physician expectations; proximity to MMC, traffic, parking • patient expectations; amenities, traffic, parking	2nd quarter, FY6
4. Document strategy for cost-effective practice start-up/expansion options at MMC.	4th quarter, FY6

Resources Required:	**Estimated Capital Costs:**
Human	Consulting: $20,000
Capital Equipment	Variable by study outcome
Facilities	Variable by study outcome

Total Estimated Capital Costs: $20,000

Responsible Department: Administration

Status Report:

APPENDIX C: SAMPLE QUESTIONNAIRES

[1-3] *MEDICAL CLINIC PATIENT SATISFACTION SURVEY*

We are conducting a survey of our clinic patients and we need your help. Please fill out the questionnaire as frankly and honestly as possible. You should not sign your name on the questionnaire to help keep your responses confidential.

For each statement below please indicate whether you strongly agree (SA), agree (A), have no opinion (NO), disagree (D), or strongly disagree (SD). Please circle one answer only.

[4]	When I called to schedule an appointment, the time I had to wait to see the doctor was reasonable.	(SA) (A) (NO) (D) (SD)
[5]	The day of my appointment, there was ample parking space.	(SA) (A) (NO) (D) (SD)
[6]	The doctor's office is conveniently located.	(SA) (A) (NO) (D) (SD)
[7]	When I arrived, the receptionist was courteous and helpful.	(SA) (A) (NO) (D) (SD)
[8]	The waiting room was comfortable and clean.	(SA) (A) (NO) (D) (SD)
[9]	My waiting time was reasonable.	(SA) (A) (NO) (D) (SD)
[10]	The examination room was clean and in order.	(SA) (A) (NO) (D) (SD)
[11]	The temperature in the examination room was comfortable.	(SA) (A) (NO) (D) (SD)
[12]	The doctor I saw showed a sincere interest in me.	(SA) (A) (NO) (D) (SD)
[13]	The doctor I saw was competent to help me.	(SA) (A) (NO) (D) (SD)
[14]	The doctor I saw took time to address all of my medical problems.	(SA) (A) (NO) (D) (SD)
[15]	The doctor took time to explain the medication he/she prescribed.	(SA) (A) (NO) (D) (SD)
[16]	The doctor I saw was courteous.	(SA) (A) (NO) (D) (SD)
[17]	The nurse who assisted my doctor was courteous and helpful.	(SA) (A) (NO) (D) (SD)
[18]	My medical needs were attended to.	(SA) (A) (NO) (D) (SD)

[19]	The financial staff was courteous and helpful.	(SA) (A) (NO) (D) (SD)
[20]	The financial staff helped me arrange payment for services.	(SA) (A) (NO) (D) (SD)
[21]	The doctor's fees were reasonable.	(SA) (A) (NO) (D) (SD)
[22]	I received follow-up care when needed from the doctor.	(SA) (A) (NO) (D) (SD)
[23]	The instructions from the doctor on prescriptions were clear.	(SA) (A) (NO) (D) (SD)
[24]	I intend to see the doctors at Quality Medical Clinic again when the need arises.	(SA) (A) (NO) (D) (SD)

Now we would like to have your comments about your experience at the clinic.

[25] What did you like *best* about your most recent visit to the clinic?

____

____

____

[26] What did you like *least* about your most recent visit to the clinic?

____

____

____

[27] What could be done to improve the service provided by the clinic?

1. ____
2. ____
3. ____
4. ____
5. ____

[28] Are there any other comments about your experience at Quality Medical Clinic that you want to share with us?

____

____

____

____

____

Now we would like to have some information about you.

Which of the following categories contains your age?
[29] _______ 0-17
[30] _______ 18-34
[31] _______ 35-49
[32] _______ 50-64
[33] _______ 65 or over

What is your marital status?
[34] _______ single
[35] _______ married
[36] _______ divorced
[37] _______ widowed

Sex:
[38] _______ male
[39] _______ female

What is the highest level of education you have completed?
[40] _______ completed elementary school
[41] _______ completed middle school
[42] _______ completed high school
[43] _______ completed some college
[44] _______ completed college
[45] _______ completed advanced degree

What is your occupation?
[46] _______ homemaker
[47] _______ student
[48] _______ laborer
[49] _______ skilled
[50] _______ professional
[51] _______ retired

Which of the following categories contains your family's annual income?
[52] _______ less than $10,000
[53] _______ $10,001-$30,000
[54] _______ $30,001-$50,000
[55] _______ $50,001-$70,000
[56] _______ $70,001-$90,000
[57] _______ $90,001 or over

Thank you for helping us with this survey. Please use the return envelope to mail the questionnaire back to us as soon as possible. The return envelope does not need a stamp.

REGIONAL MEDICAL CENTER

Dear Patient:

No organization is perfect, and hospitals are certainly no exception. We at the Regional Medical Center want to provide the best service possible, but to do so we need to know what we are doing right and what needs improvement. This means we must depend on our patients to keep us informed about how we are doing.

To do this, we need your help.

Please fill out the enclosed questionnaire as frankly and honestly as possible and return it to us. Your opinion is important to us and will be held in strictest confidence. The return envelope does not need a stamp. Thank you for your time and help.

Sincerely,

Terry James
Administrator

[1-3]

REGIONAL MEDICAL CENTER OUTPATIENT SERVICES SURVEY

INSTRUCTIONS: You recently visited our Health Center. Please rate the services you received. **Circle** the **number** that best represents your feelings. If you had no experience with a particular item, **skip** to the next question. Also **comment** on any negative or positive experience you might have had in each area. When you have completed the survey, please mail it back in the enclosed envelope. THANKS!

GENERAL QUESTIONS (fill in)

[4] 1. Date of this visit? ____________________

[5] 2. Was this your first visit as a patient to our Health Center?
_______ Yes _______ No

[6] 3. Your age? _______

[7] 4. Your sex? _______Male _______ Female

A. Registration	**very poor**	**poor**	**fair**	**good**	**very good**
[8] 1. If you spoke with the Health Center by phone, helpfulness of the person you spoke with	1	2	3	4	5
[9] 2. How easy it was to get an appointment for when you wanted	1	2	3	4	5
[10] 3. Convenience of parking	1	2	3	4	5
[11] 4. Helpfulness of the person at the registration desk	1	2	3	4	5
[12] 5. How well billing and insurance questions were handled	1	2	3	4	5
[13] 6. Comfort of the registration waiting room	1	2	3	4	5
[14] 7. Waiting time in registration	1	2	3	4	5

Comments (describe good or bad experience): ____________________

____

____

B. Lab, X-Ray, EKG	**very poor**	**poor**	**fair**	**good**	**very good**
[15] 1. Waiting time in the lab area	1	2	3	4	5
[16] 2. Courtesy of the person who took your blood	1	2	3	4	5
[17] 3. How well your blood was taken (quick, little pain)	1	2	3	4	5
[18] 4. Waiting time in the X-ray department	1	2	3	4	5
[19] 5. Courtesy of the X-ray technician	1	2	3	4	5
[20] 6. Waiting time in the EKG department	1	2	3	4	5
[21] 7. Courtesy of the EKG technician	1	2	3	4	5

Comments (describe good or bad experience): ____________________

____

____

C. Outpatient Tests and Treatments (skip to the last section if you did not use the following services): **Please circle the last service you visited, and then rate that service (circle one only):**

1. Ultrasound
2. Mammography
3. CT Scan
4. Nuclear Scan
5. Orthopedics
6. Respiratory Therapy
7. Echocardiogram
8. Physical Therapy
9. Stress Testing
10. Radiation Therapy
11. Chemotherapy
12. Oral surgery
13. Other _______ (specify)

		very poor	poor	fair	good	very good
[22]	1. Time you spent waiting in this test or treatment area	1	2	3	4	5
[23]	2. Friendliness of technicians and therapists	1	2	3	4	5
[24]	3. Friendliness of nurses who may have worked with you	1	2	3	4	5
[25]	4. Friendliness of the doctor who may have worked with you during your test or treatment	1	2	3	4	5
[26]	5. Explanations you were given by this doctor about your test or treatment	1	2	3	4	5
[27]	6. Explanations from other staff about what was being done to you	1	2	3	4	5
[28]	7. Staff concern for your comfort	1	2	3	4	5
[29]	8. Technical skill of technicians or therapists	1	2	3	4	5

Comments (describe good or bad experience): ____________________

____

____

D. Some Final Ratings of Outpatient Services

		very poor	poor	fair	good	very good
[30]	1. Staff concern for your privacy	1	2	3	4	5
[31]	2. Staff courtesy toward your family	1	2	3	4	5
[32]	3. Staff concern to keep your family informed about your test or treatment	1	2	3	4	5

[33]	4. Decor and cheerfulness of the Health Center	1	2	3	4	5
[34]	5. Cleanliness of the Health Center	1	2	3	4	5
[35]	6. How easy it was to find your way around the center	1	2	3	4	5
[36]	7. Likelihood of your recommending our outpatient services to others	1	2	3	4	5

Comments (describe good or bad experience): ____________________

____

____

THANK YOU!

[1-3] *DENTAL CLINIC PATIENT SURVEY*

We are conducting a patient survey for our dental clinic and we need your help. Please answer the questions below by circling the number of the answer that most closely corresponds to your opinion. You do not need to put your name on the questionnaire. Your answers will be combined with others to help us evaluate our services. It should take only 6-8 minutes to complete this form. Your time and cooperation are appreciated.

	Agree Strongly	Agree	Disagree Strongly	Disagree	Undecided	Don't Know
GENERAL CHARACTERISTICS OF THE CLINIC						
[4] 1. Well known generally.	5	4	3	2	1	0
[5] 2. Long time in community.	5	4	3	2	1	0
PHYSICAL CHARACTERISTICS OF THE CLINIC						
[6] 3. The clinic was clean.	5	4	3	2	1	0
[7] 4. The clinic had attractive decor.	5	4	3	2	1	0
[8] 5. The clinic had a comfortable atmosphere.	5	4	3	2	1	0
CONVENIENCE OF THE CLINIC						
[9] 6. The clinic is near where I live.	5	4	3	2	1	0
[10] 7. It was difficult to make an appointment.	5	4	3	2	1	0
[11] 8. It was difficult to find a parking place.	5	4	3	2	1	0

	Agree Strongly	Agree	Disagree Strongly	Disagree	Undecided	Don't Know
SERVICES OFFERED BY THE CLINIC						
[12] 9. Wide selection of services offered.	5	4	3	2	1	0
[13] 10. A high quality of services rendered.	5	4	3	2	1	0
CHARGES OF THE CLINIC						
[14] 11. Low compared to other clinics/dentists.	5	4	3	2	1	0
[15] 12. The billing practice is fair.	5	4	3	2	1	0
STAFF PERSONNEL (RECEPTIONIST/DENTAL ASSISTANT)						
[16] 13. The clinic personnel were courteous.	5	4	3	2	1	0
[17] 14. The clinic personnel were friendly.	5	4	3	2	1	0
[18] 15. The clinic personnel were helpful.	5	4	3	2	1	0
YOUR FRIENDS AND THE CLINIC						
[19] 16. The clinic was unknown to your friends.	5	4	3	2	1	0
[20] 17. The clinic was poorly recommended by your friends.	5	4	3	2	1	0
[21] 18. I would recommend the clinic to my friends.	5	4	3	2	1	0

[22] 19. How many times have you or a member of your family been to the clinic?

_______ first visit _______ 2-5 times
_______ 6-10 times _______ more than 10 times

[23] 20. How did you find out about the clinic?

_______ friends _______ family member
_______ clinic employee
_______ other, please explain ____________________

[24] 21. Are you a

_______ patient _______ parent/guardian of a patient

[25] 22. What, in your opinion, could be done to improve the services of the dental clinic?

____

____

NOW A FEW QUESTIONS ABOUT YOU

23. Which of the following categories contains your age?
[26] _______ 0-17
[27] _______ 18-34
[28] _______ 35-49
[29] _______ 50-64
[30] _______ 65 or over

24. What is your marital status?
[31] _______ single
[32] _______ married
[33] _______ divorced
[34] _______ widowed

25. Sex:
[35] _______ male
[36] _______ female

26. What is the highest level of education you have completed?
[37] _______ completed elementary school
[38] _______ completed middle school
[39] _______ completed high school
[40] _______ completed some college
[41] _______ completed college
[42] _______ completed advanced degree

27. What is your occupation?
    [43] _______ homemaker
    [44] _______ student
    [45] _______ laborer
    [46] _______ skilled
    [47] _______ professional
    [48] _______ retired

28. Which of the following categories contains your family's annual income?
    [49] _______ less than $10,000
    [50] _______ $10,001-$30,000
    [51] _______ $30,001-$50,000
    [52] _______ $50,001-$70,000
    [53] _______ $70,001-$90,000
    [54] _______ $90,001 or over

Thank you for helping us with this survey. Please use the return envelope to mail the questionnaire back to us as soon as possible. The return envelope does not need a stamp.

Index

American Hospital Association, 48
Assumptions, 69-71
  worksheet, 86

Browning, Robert, 87
Burke, Edmund, 55

Carroll, Lewis, 21
Columbia Healthcare Corporation, 5
Coolidge, Calvin, 35

Davis, Gary Scott, 115
Distinctive competence, 62-66,117
Drucker, Peter, 25,36,57,87

Eisenhower, Dwight, 14
Environmental analysis
  assumptions, 69-71
  example, 59-60
  external, 55-61
  internal, 61-66
  for setting objectives, 93
  significance of, 56-58
  SWOT, 66-68
  worksheet, 73-76
Evaluation and control, 129-141
  financial ratios, 134-135
  integration of planning, 130-132
  performance. *See* Performance evaluation and control
  timing of information flows, 132
  worksheet, 140-141,173-174

Event, 8
External analysis, 55-61
  assessment, 60-61
  example, 59-60
  factors, 58-59
  opportunities, 60-61
  significance of, 56-58
  threats, 60-61

Financial ratios, 134-135

Goal-setting
  challenges, 13
  importance of, 18

Health Care Organization (HCO)
  differences from the traditional business, 4
  needs of, 16-19
Health Maintenance Organization (HMO), 2,5
Health Net, 114
Holy Cross Hospital, 2,3,36
Hospital Corporation of America, 5

Internal analysis, 61-66
  financial resources, 64-65
  management and planning systems, 63-64
  marketing resources, 65
  operations resources, 65
  strengths, 62-66
  weaknesses, 62-66
  worksheet, 76-86

Lifetime Corporation, 5
Lowell, J.R., 87
Luke, 129

Managed care networks, 115
  concerns, 115-116
Managing by crisis (MBC), 90
Managing by extrapolation (MBE), 90
Managing by hope (MBH), 90
Managing by objectives (MBO), 89
  alternatives to, 90-91
  steps, 89-90
Managing by subjectives (MBS), 90
Medical Clinic
  managed care department plan, 199-203
  operations department plan, 205-209
  strategic plan, 185-197
Metropolitan Medical Center
  strategic plan, 231-241
Mission (purpose) statement
  definition, 18, 25,36
  elements of, 37-38
  evaluation, 47-48
  key points, 45-46
  reasons for, 37
  samples, 41-45
  worksheet, 51-52,149-151
  writing of, 39-41

Objectives, 37,87
  characteristics of good, 91-95
  definition, 87
  environmental analysis as basis for, 98-99
  management by, 89
  nature of, 87-90
  performance contracts, 100
  periodic review, 100-101
  purposes, 89
  reasons for failure to set, 88
  role of, 87-90
  setting, 96
Objectives *(continued)*
  suggestions for writing, 95
  types, 95-98
    funding, 97-98
    patient/client (customer), 98
    productivity, 96-97
  worksheet, 106-107,166-167
Olsten Corporation, 5
Operational plan, 28-29,109,117-120
  action plan format, 120
  communication strategy key elements, 118-119
  definition, 117
Opportunities, 60-61

Performance evaluation and control, 132-136
  establishing procedures, 136
  guidelines, 136-137
  patient/client feedback, 136
  revenue/cost controls, 133-136
  services rendered, 132-133
  worksheet, 140-141
Planning
  advantages, 8-11
  benefits, 10
  committee (team), 11-12
  definition, 7
  implementation problems, 13-15
  importance of, 5-7,15
  influence of revenue sources, 15-16
  irrelevance, 13
  long-term, 7
  objections to, 9
  place in the organization, 11-12
  primary purpose, 10
  reasons for, 10-11
  resistance to, 12-15
  short-term, 8
  significant points, 11
  strategic vs. tactical, 7
  team
    reasons for, 11-12
    responsibilities, 12
  worksheet, 32-33,147-148

Plans
  defined, 7
  strategic, 7
  tactical, 7-8
  types, 7-8
Plautus, 109
Preferred Provider Organizations (PPOs), 5
Process, 23, 30
Product, 23
Program, 8
Purpose
  definition, 25,35-36
  evaluation, 47-48
  importance of defining, 35-37
  issues to be covered, 45-46
  statement of. *See* Mission statement

Qual-Med, 114

Reed, John, 55
Regional Medical Center
  strategic plan, 211-238
Revenue sources, 15-16
Rochefoucauld, François De La, 35

Situation analysis, 55
  environmental factors for analysis, 58-60
  external, 55-56
  internal, 61-62
  opportunities assessment, 60-61
  significance of environmental considerations, 56-58
  strengths, 61-66
  threats assessment, 60-61
  weaknesses, 61-66
  worksheet, 73-86,152-165
Solomon, 35
State Penitentiary
  strategic plan, 179-183
Strategic decisions, 6,21-22
  context in which made, 22
Strategic planning
  definition, 21-22
  goal, 21
  view as a process, 30
Strategic planning process
  analysis of, 26-27
  assumptions of, 26-27
  control, 29
  definition, 6,14-15,21-23
  development, 28
  evaluation, 29
  goal, 21
  implementation, 30-31
  objectives, 22,27-28
  on-going process, 30
  operational plan, 28-29
  participation in, 30-31
  process, 23
  product, 23
  questions, 23
  steps, 24
  strategy development, 28
  systematic approach, 23
  tactical, 22
  two Ps, 23
  worksheet, 32-33
Strategos, 21
Strategy
  alternatives, 110-117
    cost leadership, 112-113
    differentiation 110-111
    focus, 111-112
  defined, 109-110
  development, 28,110
  factors influencing, 116-117
  implementation, 30-31,113
    joint ventures, 113-114
    mergers, 114-115
    strategic alliances, 113
    tactical issues, 115
  worksheet, 124-128,168-172
Strengths, 61-66
  assessing, 62-66
  benchmarks for identifying, 62

SWOT, 10,26,66-68
  alternate approach, 68
  format, 67
  goal of, 66
Syrus, Publilius, 129

Thoreau, Henry David, 109
Threats, 60-61
Toffler, Alvin, 57

UniHealth America, 2-3

Vision statement, 18,25,48-49

Wal-Mart, 61
Weaknesses, 61-66
  assessing, 62-66
  benchmarks for, 62
Welch, John F., 1
Worksheets
  evaluation and control, 140-141
  mission statement, 51-54
  objectives, 106-107
  planning process, 32-33
  situation analysis, 76-86
  strategy development, 124-128